Another
BLUE STRAWBERY

George Stavrinos

Scented sighs of curried moons,
Of parsnips, orange, and lime,
A breeze of brandy, quails' egg candy,
And a mould of jellied thyme.
Tangerines and legs of veal,
Plump mushrooms porcelain white,
A sigh of onion quite perfectly done
In a sauce for Saturday night.
Melons, cheese, and pheasant's breast,
Fiddlehead ferns in spring,
An Ovaltine mousse, frogs' legs, and goose,
A Wizard can cook everything!

Another BLUE STRAWBERY

More Brilliant Cooking Without Recipes

JAMES HALLER

THE HARVARD COMMON PRESS
HARVARD AND BOSTON, MASSACHUSETTS

The Harvard Common Press
535 Albany Street
Boston, Massachusetts 02118

Library of Congress Cataloging in Publication Data

Haller, James.
   Another Blue Strawbery.
   Includes index.
   1. Cookery. 2. Blue Strawbery (Restaurant)
I. Title.
TX715.H18   1983   641.5   83–12727
ISBN 0–916782–47–6
ISBN 0–916782–46–8 (pbk.)

Edited by Leslie A. Hanna
Illustrations by Bob Marstall
Cover design and frontispiece by George Stavrinos

10 9 8 7 6 5 4 3 2

ISBN 0-916782-47-6   HC
ISBN 0-916782-46-8   PB

For
James Earl and Mildred Dominick Heien,
my mother and father,
who gave me an appetite for living.
I gratefully and lovingly dedicate my best
in return for their having given me theirs.

Contents

Acknowledgments   xi

Introduction   1

Your Own Butter   5

Appetizers   10

Soups   19

Salads and Dressings   30

Fish   38

Birds   46

Meat   56

Vegetables   69

Fast Foods   79

Sauces for a Crowd   94

After Dinner   103

Menus   112

Index   121

A NOTE FROM THE PUBLISHER

Why another Blue Strawbery? Portsmouth's Strawbery Banke was one of the earliest Pilgrim settlements in New Hampshire and in America. When the area was restored in the early 1970s, the Blue Strawbery restaurant was among its first tenants, and James Haller became its resident wizard. The restaurant's founders adopted the original Pilgrim spelling of "strawbery"; and they took from their forebears, too, a love of fresh, native foods, prepared simply but with a dollop of something extra—a little wild, perhaps, a little . . . blue.

Those who know the first collection of brilliant Blue Strawbery cookery were introduced in its pages to Jim Haller's concept of cooking with only the most general guidelines, or "roadmaps," as he calls them. Besides explaining how to make the unforgettable dishes served at the Blue Strawbery, Haller suggests fascinating and limitless variations that can be conjured up with a quick wit and whatever happens to be in the kitchen. To those who catch the spirit of the Blue Strawbery, Haller's "roadmaps" will be much more than recipes; they will be takeoff points for the imagination. We present them with the utmost pleasure for your delectation.

Acknowledgments

I would like to express my continued gratitude and appreciation to my partners Mark John Burke and Gene Brown, who through their constant loyalty have given me the freedom to do my best; to Thomas O'Brien, who keeps my kitchen well stocked with sunshine; to Donna Stafford, Eddie Wydra, Raymond LaVigne, Brad Jewett, Pam Oates, Jerry Daniels, Chris Remignetti, Lisa Merchant, John Shoos, Annie Pease, and Brett Kurzwell, who all clean and cut and chop and stir and lift and carry and present my creations; to Phillip McGuire, whose perfect taste and commitment gave me the time to write this book; to Mary Ann Roberge, who plowed through a lot of illegible nonsense and turned it into typewritten pages on schedule; for dear Leslie Hanna, who uncomplainingly drove hundreds of miles a week to share her editorial expertise— you are a gift; for Doctor Chuck Spezzano and Doctor Elisabeth Kübler-Ross, who one incredible evening in Oregon turned the lights back on in my kitchen.

Another Blue Strawbery

Introduction

We never really change; we only become more of who we are. When my first Blue Strawbery cookbook appeared in 1976, some readers were taken by surprise, even shocked. They said I would set the cooking world on its ear with my carefree advice to "throw away the rules." My purpose was, and continues to be, simply to stimulate people to delight themselves and their guests by unfettering their culinary imaginations.

I am as deeply committed as ever to the principles of freshness and wholesomeness of food for the body, and innovative combinations of flavors and textures for the spirit. I still champion the anything-can-taste-good cause. But like the rest of you I have matured in the last seven years, and so has my cooking. It isn't that I have changed direction, only that I see the path more clearly.

The now widespread awareness that Americans eat more red meat than is probably good for them has not been lost on me, for example; I discuss this subject further in my meat chapter. The rapid inflation that undermines our food budgets has made me a devoted fan of the food processor as well as the blender; with them I make my own pestos and flavored butters, oils, vinegars, and coffee, any of which would be expensive if bought prepared and packaged. I am also growing my own fresh herbs, and, instead of searching far and wide for exotic edibles, more and more I find I'm looking close to home. I hold fast to the economic wisdom of fresh native foods, locally grown or produced. I think food processing and packaging reflects our inflation-wracked economy in which we are continually paying more for less—more for water, sugar, salt, and advertising than for substance and nourishment. You'll find no convenience foods called for in these pages, except artichoke hearts and chicken bouillon.

You *will* find "Fast Food," however. The unending struggle to beat the clock, which makes us think we have no time to eat, let alone cook, is the force behind this aptly named chapter. The enthusiastic response to my eight-minute cooking spots on local Boston television shows that people still want "real" food, even when it has to be fast.

But the old Shaker approach of "taking the ordinary and making it extraordinary" has probably come to be the single most enjoyable and enlightening principle of cooking for me. Anyone can be brilliant with a pound of truffles from Italy and creamed goats' cheese from France, but to search out your own backyard for dandelions, fiddlehead ferns, and day lily buds to garnish a sherried cream of radish soup made with neighborhood goats' milk takes a little more imagination (especially if you live in the city).

My successes in the kitchen have never hinged on what ingredients a recipe called for, but rather on my own flexibility in dealing with what I had on hand. Instead of letting a particular array of ingredients dampen your spirits and style, allow it to kindle your awareness of what could be. I guess if there is any secret to my cooking, it's that I always seek out new possibilities.

The recipes I've included here in my second cookbook are for old favorites, new favorites, and even a few things I've yet to try out in the restaurant. A whole new chapter is devoted to making your own butters. Personalized vinegars and oils dress up the salad chapter this time around, and "entertaining made easy" is the essence of a new twist to my sauce chapter. A final chapter, "After Dinner," is highlighted by my "formula" for cheesecake and ideas for flavored coffees.

As I wrote in my first cookbook, each of my recipes is really only a proposal, a foundation on which to base your own experiments in the kitchen. The last thing I would want is for you to feel restricted simply because you don't have a pound of goose livers or canary tongues. The recipes are meant to inspire rather than intimidate, to poke you in the tastebuds and awaken the "spoon wizard" within you. In this respect my philosophy hasn't changed at all. It is and always will be "entirely up to you."

Your Own Butter

I was first inspired to make my own butter for the restaurant while vacationing in California. One is always inspired in California, if only to homesickness. The possibility of homemade butter opened a whole new area of cooking for me. Not only did I find that I could churn ten pounds in about fifteen minutes using a food processor, but the incredible luxury of cooking with my own butter was an unexpected satisfaction. We keep inventing machines to "make the work easier"; the problem is that everyone has forgotten what the work is. Making butter is part of that work.

Making butter is quite simple. Using the large chopper blade in your food processor, pour in a quart of cream and just let it go. It will become whipped and then just keep getting thicker and thicker until it finally separates. Put it all into a mixing bowl, squeeze the liquid from the fat with your (clean) hands, and there you are—a lump of butter. I have found that the best results occur if you let the cream sit in the refrigerator for a week before you churn it and then let it warm almost to room temperature.

Now, a quart of heavy cream usually runs about $1.74. From that quart I churn anywhere from one and a quarter pounds to one and three-quarters pounds of butter. Whereas a pound of store-bought butter usually costs about $1.80, a pound of my home-churned butter costs between $1.00 and $1.40—I save about four thousand dollars a year! Won't the dairy people love that? Furthermore, the skim milk that's left is sweeter, more wholesome, and far more delicious than any I could buy in a supermarket. It could only be fresher if the cow were making it herself.

That skim milk goes into soups, sauces, and custards, and no one knows that what they are eating is good for them.

Of course there are those who, at this moment, are probably concerned about all that fat, cholesterol, and other negative things the medical world has told us about butter. But let's not neglect the positive side of this natural food. It does provide some necessary nutrients, such as vitamin A and the minerals calcium, phosphorus, potassium, and sodium.

I'm not suggesting that everyone should sit around eating pounds of butter at a meal. It *is* fattening, and anything in excess is unhealthy. The first week I made butter I gained three pounds—tasting, constantly tasting. But now that I've done the tasting for you, all you have to do is whip it up for a special occasion.

WHAT TO DO WITH YOUR LUMP OF BUTTER

Break it into one-inch pieces and throw it back into the processor. This is the point where you make the butter into any fantasy that pleases you. I generally add about two tablespoons of fresh herbs and a little nutmeg, black pepper, and salt. Spin it just long enough to smooth the herbs and soften the butter into a "whip." You now have what is probably the most wonderful herb butter you've ever eaten.

After you learn the herbs, the rest comes easily. Ripe pears whipped into fresh butter, or blackberries, or maple syrup, or lobster meat. The possibilities are endless. Imagine whipping a handful of wild strawberries into your butter and squeezing it through a pastry bag onto French toast points that have been sautéed in Grand Marnier and dusted with vanilla sugar. That, and a cup of coffee, would be a wonderful way to celebrate the first morning of a romance—or the last.

Liqueurs mixed with butter, or vegetables, curry, chocolate, olives? Naturally there's garlic. But how about juices—lime, lemon, or orange? Or even fish;—smoked salmon butter would seem lovely to me on baked oysters, drizzled over whole mushrooms sauteed in cognac, or spread on little crustless sandwiches made of lemon-soaked cucumber slices. Caviar butter seems pedestrian, but maybe if you spooned it onto cream cheese–covered wheat thins or Ritz crackers or Uneeda biscuits you could start a trend.

Here are a few simple recipes to help make any occasion more special. Start with your lump of home-churned.

Nasturtium Butter

Squeeze and drain butter, break into small pieces, and return to your processor. Add four to six nasturtium blossoms and either two tablespoons of powdered sugar or one teaspoon of salt. Try it without any seasoning, too! A sweet nasturtium butter on whipped cream biscuits, cinnamon-raisin toast, or hot corn muffins would be welcome at any meal. Unsweetened, it is delicious for hot salmon, boiled lobster, fiddlehead ferns, bread-and-butter sandwiches, or even biscuits.

Obviously we cannot get nasturtiums all year long. You could also use violets and even squash or pumpkin blossoms. In fact, day lilies in bud would work. All else failing, you might want to try half a tablespoon of rose or orange blossom water.

Sweet Curry Butter

After returning the cubes of butter to the processor, add two tablespoons of a good curry powder (I use

(Sweet Curry Butter)

Madras) and two tablespoons of white sugar. I some-times sweeten this instead with honey or maple syrup; either mixed with curry ends up reminiscent of mo-lasses.

Curried Pear Butter

To the fresh butter (drained, cubed, and returned to processor), add one very ripe pear, seeded and cored, but unpeeled, and one tablespoon of curry pow-der. This is an elegant toast topping for out-of-town guests.

Mint Butter

Add one-fourth cup chopped fresh mint and the juice of one lime to your lump of home-churned butter. Highly recommended for salmon, but don't stop there!

Cinnamon Orange Butter

Process your butter with two tablespoons of frozen orange concentrate and one tablespoon each of or-ange marmalade and cinnamon.

Nutmeg and Basil Butter

Add six tablespoons of minced fresh basil and one tablespoon each of ground nutmeg and black pepper to your lump of homemade butter.

Garlic Butter Supreme

Process with about a pound and a half of fresh butter: eight garlic cloves, four tablespoons of pure olive oil, six tablespoons of Parmesan cheese, the juice of one lemon, and one tablespoon each of fresh basil, chives, marjoram, and black pepper. When smoothly blended, use in pie dough for quiche or on French or Italian bread for a great garlic toast. And what could be bet-ter for cooking fish, shellfish, chicken, or vegetables?

The formula for inspired butters is simple. For fruit flavors, use three-fourths to a whole cup of fruit for each pound and a half of butter. With herbs, work with teaspoons and tablespoons, and for sweet butters, add half a cup of "sweet." If you try liqueurs, one-quarter cup for the same pound and a half of butter should do it.

The whole idea of these butters is that you'll use them for all the ordinary things for which you need butter. Mushrooms sauteed in pumpkin butter, chicken breast prepared in blueberry-pepper butter, asparagus in a gingered violet butter, or the simple English muffin made romantic when spread with a rose butter. Try a half cup of smoked salmon and a half cup of cream cheese processed with your fresh butter—it now seems destined for an onion bagel. This isn't traditional, of course, but "traditional" often only means unprogressive.

The truly adventurous will use flavored butters for croissants, brioches, and butter pastries. My friends at Portsmouth's Ceres Bakery are excited about this idea, and they make the best croissant in all of North America. I'd like to see—and taste—a nasturtium butter croissant.

These Indian cornmeal doughnuts could be made with a flavored butter for a weekend morning treat. Imagine dipping them, hot from bear or bison grease, into a cup of sassafras tea! It's all part of our own Renaissance—of native American cooking!

Indian Doughnuts

Pour one and a half cups of scalded milk over two cups of cornmeal. While it cools, sift together two cups of flour, a cup and a half of sugar, a tablespoon of baking powder, a tablespoon of cinnamon or nutmeg (or spice of your choice), and a teaspoon of salt. Add the sifted dry ingredients to the cooled milk and cornmeal. Stir well, then whisk in a cup of melted flavored butter and three beaten eggs. If necessary, add more flour to make the dough firm enough to handle, but keep it as soft as possible. Knead lightly. Roll out on a floured board; shape with a floured doughnut cutter. Let doughnuts stand fifteen minutes before deep-frying. Drain; sprinkle with powdered sugar.

Appetizers

Appetizers are supposed to whet one's appetite for the entire dinner. I think they should also satisfy a taste by themselves. Appetizers are usually perfect all alone if you're on a weight-loss program. A cup of onion soup with baked or raw oysters and a green salad make a great meal, filled with nutrients and few calories. Think of an appetizer as a small one-dish meal—a light brunch or luncheon or a simple supper. The rich use of herbs and novel combinations help a small portion to satisfy an eyes-bigger-than-the-waistline appetite.

ARTICHOKE HEARTS

Cooking one hundred artichokes at a time so I can use just the hearts is more of a challenge than I care to think about. There are times when I steam the entire artichoke and serve it with some fantastic flavored butter (see "Your Own Butter") for leaf dipping.

Usually, though, I want just the heart, so I simply open a can. Call me what you like. I admit on occasion I'm lazy—but never too lazy to whip up Hearts of Artichoke in a Sherried Havarti Custard for a guest.

Artichoke Hearts in Havarti and Sherry Custard

Line a pie pan or baking dish with a crust (try the butter crust recipe that follows). Cover the bottom with artichoke hearts. Process a cup of Havarti cheese and a half cup of dry sherry with four eggs, half a cup of light cream, a tablespoon of flour, and a dash each of tarragon and black pepper. Pour this custard mixture over the artichokes, and bake at 325° for forty-five minutes.

Crust (makes two): In a food processor, work two-thirds cup of butter (cut into one-inch cubes) into two and one-quarter cups of flour and a teaspoon of baking powder. With the machine running, slowly dribble in one-third cup ice-cold water. The dough should form a ball. Remove, knead a few times, cut in two, and roll out one (or both) crusts. Do not use flour during the rolling unless absolutely necessary.

Artichoke Hearts in Brie Custard

Line a pie pan, baking dish, or individual server with the butter crust in the preceding recipe. Cover the bottom with artichoke hearts, pour in the cheese custard, and bake at 325° for forty-five minutes.

Custard: Blend a cup of Brie with four eggs, half a cup of vermouth, three peeled garlic cloves, the juice of one lemon, half a teaspoon of tarragon, and a taste of white pepper and salt.

LIVER

I often choose goose livers for my appetizers. Generally they are found frozen in five-pound containers, but I prefer them fresh. If you can get fresh goose livers, and you might if you order them, you are in luck. In France, I am told, they force feed geese stuck in boxes so they can't go anywhere. The lack of exercise seems to guarantee a rich, oversized liver. Chicken livers are strong-flavored in comparison, rabbit livers are too cloying, and duck livers are often chalky. But goose liver—a true delicacy.

Goose Livers in Cognac Cream with Duxelles

Heat about six tablespoons of butter in a frying pan until it sizzles; add a pound of goose livers. Sprinkle them generously with salt, black pepper, garlic, thyme, paprika, and chopped fresh parsley. Brown quickly on both sides, then flambé with a half-cup splash of fine cognac. Remove livers, and add a tablespoon of flour to the pan drippings for thickening. Slowly stir in a pint of heavy cream. Transfer to a blender, adding one egg, and whirl until smooth. Return to the heat and slowly warm until the sauce is velvety thick. Season with salt and pepper and fold in duxelles. Arrange goose livers in ramekins, add sauce, and bake twelve minutes at 400°. Or, bake the livers and sauce in one large dish and serve on toast points.

Duxelles: Mince two pounds of fresh mushrooms (or shred in a food processor). Place them in the center of a clean white dish towel, (who has cheesecloth around the house?) and, holding the four corners in one hand, twist the center part tighter and tighter until you've squeezed as much juice from the mushrooms as possible. (Save this juice for other sauces.) Melt one cup of butter in a frying pan, then add the squeezed mushroom pieces. Let them cook slowly until they've absorbed the butter. You now have duxelles; add it to sauces, soups, stuffings, quiches, or any-thing you might invent.

Goose Livers in Marmalade and Brandy Sauce

Prepare the sauce first by blending half a cup of brandy with a quarter cup of Grey Poupon (or mus-tard of your choice) and a cup of marmalade—or-ange, lime, lemon, or grapefruit. Heat six tablespoons of butter in a frying pan, add a pound of goose livers, and season with salt, black pepper, garlic, thyme, paprika, and chopped fresh parsley. Brown the livers quickly on both sides, then pour in the sauce. As the livers sizzle on high heat, keep turning them until the sauce forms a glaze. Serve.

Two variations on this goose liver theme are orange marma-lade with yellow mustard and crème de cassis, and grapefruit mar-malade with Dijon mustard and Frangelico.

Goose Livers with Artichoke Hearts in a Champagne and Bacon Sauce

Fry a half pound of chopped bacon until crisp, season-ing the meat while it's cooking with black pepper, garlic, basil, and parsley. Drain, discarding the grease, and set the bacon bits aside. In the same pan melt about six tablespoons of butter until sizzling, then throw in a pound of goose livers. Brown on both sides, seasoning with salt, pepper, garlic, thyme, paprika, and chopped fresh parsley. Remove livers and stir two tablespoons of flour into the pan drippings to make a paste. Add one cup of champagne and two cups of heavy cream. Stirring, bring to a simmer. When sauce thickens, transfer it to a blender with an egg and whir till smooth. If sauce seems too thin, add a touch of flour; if too thick, a little more cream. Return to the pan and simmer to cook any added flour. Add reserved bacon and salt and black pepper to taste. Ar-range cooked goose livers with artichoke hearts in ramekins or in a large bake-and-serve dish, bathe with sauce, and bake at 400° for fifteen minutes. Serve on toast points, with biscuits, or alone.

Goose Liver Pâté Brown a pound of goose livers in six tablespoons of sizzling butter, seasoning them while cooking with salt, black pepper, garlic, thyme, paprika, and chopped fresh parsley. Crisp-fry a half pound of chopped bacon, seasoning it too with black pepper, garlic, basil, and parsley. Drain on absorbent paper. Prepare a half cup of duxelles (page 12), a half pound of cooked and chopped veal (preferably leftover), and a two-minute egg. Put all this (livers, bacon, duxelles, veal, egg) in a food processor along with one-quarter cup chopped scallions, two tablespoons heavy cream, the juice of one lemon, four tablespoons cognac, some black pepper and salt, and one tablespoon each of chopped garlic, basil, tarragon, and thyme. Process with the chopper blade only long enough to make a smooth pâté. Press into a buttered springform pan and chill. Remove sides of pan when ready to serve, top with sour cream, and decorate the edges with overlapping orange slices.

MUSSELS AND TOPPINGS

Mussels are just about the last of the great gifts of the sea, and that's only because so many people refuse to eat them. The more they catch on, the higher the price gets, and the fewer you begin to find on your own. But mussels are still plentiful, and they are easier to harvest than clams. Since they usually hang out in groups, you can find a lot in a short time. On occasion you can buy them shucked. Mussels are said to be slightly aphrodisiac—the perfect American food.

Figure six fresh (tightly closed) mussels per person (throw in a few extra in case some don't open). Clean, then drop them into boiling water. Cover and steam for about two minutes—just long enough to open the shells. Discard any that don't open. Remove the black beards; separate and discard one half of each shell. Lay the other halves, with the meat attached, on a cookie sheet. Fill with any of the following butters or toppings (or sauce of your choice), and bake at 500° for eight to ten minutes. Or broil until lightly charred, about four to six minutes.

Sambuca Herb Butter

Blend just until thoroughly mixed: one cup melted butter, one-quarter cup **Sambuca**, one teaspoon of salt, the juice of one lemon, and one tablespoon each of black pepper, chopped scallions, chives, basil, marjoram, parsley, and garlic.

Strawberry–Black Pepper Topping

Chop one pint of strawberries by hand into a bowl. Add two tablespoons each of chopped onion, white vinegar, and bacon grease. Add one tablespoon each of coarse-ground black pepper and honey. Stir well and leave for fifteen minutes before using as a topping for mussels.

Sweet Pickle, Anchovy, and Green Chartreuse Topping

Mince a can of flat anchovies with a half cup of chopped sweet gherkins, a half cup of minced scallions, the juice of one lemon, a quarter cup of green chartreuse, one tablespoon of black pepper, and two tablespoons each of hot mustard and olive oil.

Peach Lobster Butter

Boil one average-sized lobster (one and a half pounds) just long enough to turn the shell to orange. Shred the meat in a food processor, or mince by hand (you'll get the same result, but it will take more time and work). Thoroughly blend lobster meat and one mashed ripe peach (with skin) into a cup of softened but-

(Peach Lobster Butter) ter. Mix in a quarter cup of chopped scallions, the juice of one lemon, a tablespoon of minced garlic, one-half teaspoon of Tabasco, two tablespoons of chopped fresh parsley, and salt and black pepper to taste. I also like to add two tablespoons of prepared lobster base, but that is optional. If you prepare this entire mixture in a food processor, process only until well blended, not pureed.

Curried Duxelles in Brandy Topping Prepare one cup duxelles (page 12), adding two tablespoons of chopped onions to the cooking mushrooms. Blend the duxelles into a half cup of softened butter. Mix in one and a half tablespoons of curry powder, four tablespoons of brandy, the juice of one lemon, and salt and pepper to taste.

This is not the final word on mussel toppings. Try "Fast Spaghetti Sauce" or a pesto, both described in the chapter headed "Fast Food." They are great over snails also, as are any of the flavored butters described in the chapter "Your Own Butter." Or you might try, naturally, any combination of foodstuffs that stimulates your own palate. What makes your mouth water?

Cold Smoked Mussels in Sour Cream and Onions To one pound of smoked mussels add half a cup of fine-sliced onion, two tablespoons of wine vinegar, and one tablespoon of brown sugar. Marinate the mussels for an hour, then fold them with the marinade into three cups of sour cream. Serve on lettuce leaves.

CONCHS

Conch is another unusual shellfish that makes an appealing appetizer. You probably think immediately of the large shells people hold to their ear to listen to the ocean—these are not the conchs

I'm talking about. The ones I use are only two to four inches long. The shells do resemble the larger ones, which makes them so attractive to serve. The best way to procure small conchs may be to ask your fishmonger to find them; they are often caught in lobster traps.

Stuffed Conchs

Steam washed conchs for thirty to forty-five minutes Drain them, and discard the "foot," the part closest to you. Remove the meat with a fork and fill the shell halfway with a stuffing. Push the meat back into the shell, add more stuffing, and bake at 400° for about fifteen minutes.

Garlic Spinach Stuffing: Add two tablespoons of pure olive oil to a half cup of melted butter in a large skillet. Toss in half a pound of trimmed, minced spinach and half a cup of chopped garlic; stir-fry until the spinach wilts. Stir in half a cup of bread crumbs, one-fourth cup of grated Parmesan, two tablespoons of lemon juice, one tablespoon of black pepper, and salt to taste.

Instead of spinach in the stuffing, you might substitute half a cup of chopped green tomatoes, mushrooms, or duxelles (page 12).

RABBIT

The first time I had a fresh-dressed rabbit delivered to the restaurant, I almost quit cooking then and there. It looked like a cat, and I could have sworn that I saw one of the little legs kick. I had to ask Raymond, a French Canadian (French Canadians know about eating rabbit), to cut it apart for me. Once I saw how simple it was, I never hesitated again. Go out and get yourself a rabbit and a French Canadian—you'll have a nice time.

Rabbit in Orange Barbecue Sauce

Most average-sized rabbits can be cut nicely into six pieces—two front and two hind legs and the back, cut in half. Rub these pieces with olive oil and sprinkle them with salt, black pepper, garlic, thyme, and paprika. Lay them in a baking dish, set a few bay leaves on top, and bake uncovered at 500° for twenty minutes. Douse with a cup of white wine, cover, reduce heat to 450°, and cook thirty minutes more. Then drain the pan juices into a blender and add one cup of frozen orange concentrate, a half cup of catsup, a quarter cup each of maple syrup and wine vinegar, and two tablespoons of minced garlic. Blend well and brush generously on the rabbit pieces. Return them, uncovered, to a 450° oven. Baste often as you roast for a final twenty minutes.

Rabbit Almondine in Mustard Maple Syrup

Prepare rabbit and begin roasting as directed in the preceding recipe. Instead of draining pan juices into a blender, just mix them well with a cup of Dijon mustard and a cup of maple syrup. Stir in a half cup of slivered almonds. Use this sauce to baste the rabbit during the final twenty minutes of roasting.

Soups

Soup is a warm welcome. When someone is arriving late at night, having a pot of hot soup waiting is one of the loveliest gestures a host can make.

Not long ago my friend and I took a ten thousand–mile journey through the United States and Canada, traveling mainly by train and ferry. The story of the Amtrak leg could be titled, "A Dirty Window to the World." The food was a disappointment, as was the lack of both courtesy and simple hospitality.

What a difference on the Canadian side! Our first taste was the magnificent breakfast buffet offered on the morning ferry from Seattle to Victoria. And the food on the Canadian train, though far from elegant, was incredibly superior to that served on the American counterpart. Any meal tastes better prepared by loving rather than resentful hands.

Meeting four lovely people from New Brunswick was the highlight of our cross-continental trek. The six of us shared the journey, and a sleeper, all the way from Vancouver to Montreal. Three thousand miles together forged our friendship.

My friend and I were soon on our way to visit these four on the Island of Whitehead, three hours out into the Canadian Maritimes. The ten-hour trip from our home in Maine included a ride on a ferry that moved so low in the water you could reach down and get your hand wet.

The four—Beulah, Ted, Cline, and Ina—welcomed us at the landing, and we walked to their house together. The kitchen table was set with steaming bowls of soup, homemade bread, strong Canadian tea, and a truly wonderful raisin pie. But the soup! It was one of the most brilliant fish stews I've ever tasted—better, in fact, than any chowder I've ever made myself.

In the morning I watched Ina knead, roll, and butter the dough for yeast biscuits while Beulah brewed coffee and spread toast with homemade preserves. These wonderful women, who smelled so clean and looked so neat, who always smiled and only spoke well of others, reminded me of the kind of woman who used to hug you against her apron when you were a kid and—just by the way she talked to you—made you feel good and loved, as if you were somebody.

For people my age, those aunts and grandmothers have long since vanished, and I had thought women like them were all gone. But there, as a welcome guest at that kitchen table on Whitehead Island, I saw that they weren't—and somehow, neither was my youth. This chapter on soups is dedicated to Ina Zwicker.

CHOWDERS

Ina Zwicker's Whitehead Island Chowder

Melt four tablespoons of butter in a soup pan; add one cup each of chopped onions and diced potatoes. Cover with water and boil until the potatoes soften. Then add one cup each of boned fresh whitefish, uncooked lobster, and scallops. Simmer until all the fish is cooked, about eight minutes. Stir in two large cans (about three cups) of evaporated milk, heated, and another four tablespoons of butter. Season to taste with salt and black pepper and serve, topping each bowl with a lump of butter. Simple enough, and probably the best chowder I've ever eaten!

Baked Salmon Bisque

Combine four tablespoons of butter in a soup pot with a thin-sliced leek, a quarter cup of flour, and one cup each of fish stock, dry sherry, and diced potatoes. Simmer until the potatoes are soft, and then blend in two batches, adding half a blenderful of light cream for each half a blenderful of soup base. Meanwhile, bake a salmon fillet (about two pounds) at 400° for twelve minutes. Flake the fish off the bones, and arrange it in either individual bake-and-serve dishes or in one large one. Fill with the cream soup mixture, sprinkle lightly with buttered bread crumbs, and bake in a 400° oven for fifteen minutes.

Sherried Mussel Cream Soup

Drop three pounds of cleaned mussels into boiling water and boil just until they open. Discard any shells that do not open during cooking. Remove the beards from the rest and discard them; pluck the meat from each mussel and set it aside. In a soup pot combine a stick of butter, a quarter cup of flour, an eight-ounce bottle of clam juice, a cup of diced potato, a cup of dry sherry (Amontillado is what I use), a quart of light cream, and a half cup of chopped shallots. Bring all this to a boil, then simmer until potatoes are soft. Blend entire mixture until velvety smooth. Add cooked mussels, a handful of fresh chopped parsley, and salt and pepper to taste. Simmer fifteen minutes and serve.

Smoked Mussels in Sherried Tomato Cream

Simmer together (until tomatoes cook down): a half stick of butter, a half cup of flour, six ripe tomatoes (remove the ends only), a small can of tomato paste, one cup of dry sherry, eight ounces of clam juice or Clamato, one tablespoon of black pepper, three cups of light cream, and one tablespoon each of fresh basil, marjoram, and thyme. Then blend the entire mixture until smooth, adding a little flour if it needs to be thicker. (If you do add flour, return to the heat to simmer for a few minutes.) Stir in a pint of smoked mussels and keep warm. Serve, floating a spoonful of sherry on each portion.

I must admit that I'm surprised at my great love for creamy fish soups. I can remember when the thought of mixing fish and milk would have sent me out of the room. Thank goodness I've managed to make definite progress in at least one area of my life.

Chowder doesn't have to mean fish. What makes a soup a chowder to me is the combination of pork fat, potatoes, and milk. But you can turn anything you want into a chowder. Have you ever had fiddlehead fern chowder, curried apple chowder, or cinnamon pumpkin chowder?

Artichoke Heart and Corn Chowder

Fry a half pound of bacon until crisp, then drain. Crumble the bacon and set it aside. Into a soup pot add two cups of diced potatoes, a medium thin-sliced onion, a half stick of butter, and the fresh kernels from two ears of corn. Cover with water and simmer until the potatoes are soft. Add a quart of light cream, the bacon bits, and one cup of dry white wine. Add salt and black pepper to taste and stir in a can of artichoke hearts that have been drained and pulled apart. Simmer to warm through, then serve.

Beet Green– Buttermilk Chowder

In a soup pot combine a half stick of butter, a thin-sliced medium leek, one cup of diced potatoes, a half pound of crisp crumbled bacon, a cup of white wine, a quart of buttermilk, and salt and black pepper to taste. Bring to a boil, then simmer until the potatoes are soft. Add three cups of chopped raw beet greens. Blend two cups of this mixture until smooth; return it to the pot and simmer about fifteen minutes longer before serving.

(Beet Green–Buttermilk Chowder)

CREAM SOUPS

I finally have an herb garden; I grow forty-seven kinds of herbs. Ten are for cooking—who could dispute the appeal of the scent and taste of green, pungent herbs? The others I think about and taste and learn about—their medicinal properties, their psychic effects, legends about them, even the possibilities of an herb-vegetable combination which would help heal an ailing body.

Combine in a soup pot: a stick of butter, two cups of diced potatoes, a raw egg, half a cup of chopped scallions, one quart of light cream, a cup of May wine, a teaspoon of black pepper, and one tablespoon each of fresh basil, marjoram, thyme, summer savory, and tarragon. Simmer until the potatoes are soft; then blend, adding one more egg, until velvet. Serve hot or chilled.

Herb and May Wine Summer Cream Soup

Prepare the cream soup base first: Throw into a soup pot a stick of butter, a cup of diced potatoes (I generally peel them, since potato peels tend to make the soup gummy), a half cup of chopped shallots (or leeks or onions), two tablespoons of chicken bouillon, one tablespoon of nutmeg, and a teaspoon each of dill and white pepper. Splash in a cup of dry white wine and a cup or so of water, just enough to submerge the

Cream of Fiddlehead Fern Soup

(Cream of Fiddlehead Fern Soup)

vegetables. Simmer until the potatoes are soft. Blend the entire mixture, adding two eggs, until velvety.

For this variation of cream soup, wash three cups of fiddlehead ferns, removing the brown fuzzy covering (simple if done under a strong stream of water). Chop the ferns into bite-sized bits, and add them to the cream soup. Simmer, stirring often, until the ferns are cooked, about forty-five minutes. Serve.

Curried Asparagus Cream Soup

Chop the tips from one and a half pounds of fresh asparagus; set them aside. Put the rest of the stalks in a soup pot with a half cup of chopped leeks, a cup of diced potatoes, half a stick of butter, a quarter cup of flour, one cup of dry white wine, two tablespoons of curry powder and a quart of light cream. Bring to a boil, then blend smooth. Return the puree to the pot and stir in the reserved tips. Simmer until the tips are cooked to your liking.

Peanut Butter and Orange Soup

Simmer the following together until the carrots are done: a half cup each of chopped onions and carrots, two tablespoons of chicken bouillon, one peeled orange, one bay leaf, one cup of dry white wine, a half cup of chunk-style peanut butter, two tablespoons of chopped chives, a quart of light cream, a quarter cup of flour, and salt and white pepper to taste. Blend until smooth, pour into a soup dish, and garnish with slivered almonds. Serve.

Vatican Vichyssoise

Into a soup pot put one stick of butter, one cup of diced potatoes, a half cup of sliced leeks, one cup of white wine, a half cup of flour, two tablespoons of chopped chives, three tablespoons of beef bouillon, and one quart of light cream. Simmer until the potatoes are soft, then blend until velvety. Remove the casing from one link of kielbasa and break bite-sized pieces into the soup. Simmer thirty minutes, stirring often. Serve.

(Vatican Vichyssoise)

The idea for the two radish soups that follow came from an old Shaker recipe for a spinach mold filled with creamed radishes. What wonderful cooks the Shakers were! Their food not only makes the most of commonplace, inexpensive ingredients, but makes the fullest use of nutritional value. One of the truly great gifts that my cooking has brought me was the opportunity to meet Eldress Bertha Lindsey and Eldress Gertrude Soule of the Canterbury Shakers in New Hampshire.

I had always thought it would be wonderful to wander off to the hillsides in India and seek out holy men just to hear what they might have to say. Though that fantasy had never materialized, there I was one incredible October afternoon, sitting on a hillside in New Hampshire and having lunch with the Eldresses Bertha and Gertrude, their friend Jenny, and dog Penny. We shared a blue flower-chive omelet that was six inches high, some yeast-risen squash biscuits, and a rose-scented apple pie made by Eldress Bertha's own hands (with a little help from Jenny). As I sat there with these ladies who were so dear and good and kind, their eyes such a clear blue and their welcome so genuine, I knew that hillsides were hillsides, whether in India or New Hampshire.

Cream of Radish Soup

Into a soup pot add a half stick of butter, a half cup of chopped scallions, one cup of diced potatoes, one cup of dry white wine, two tablespoons of chicken bouillon, one tablespoon of ground nutmeg, some white pepper, and one quart of light cream. Simmer until the potatoes are soft. Then blend smooth, adding a touch of flour if more thickening is needed. Into another pan thin-slice a pound of red radishes, then boil them until soft in enough water to cover. Drain; add the radishes to the cream soup. Simmer fifteen minutes and serve.

Champagne and Radish Cream Soup

Whir in a blender on highest speed until smooth: two cups of champagne, a half cup of flour, a half stick of butter, one chopped leek (about half a cup), two tablespoons chicken bouillon, and a teaspoon each of white pepper and nutmeg (preferably fresh-ground). Pour into a soup pot and bring to a simmer, stirring often. Add two cups of thin-sliced radishes and simmer one hour, still stirring frequently. Sprinkle with salt and black pepper. Serve piping hot or refrigerate for a full day and serve cold. Garnish with fresh parsley.

Goose Livers in Cognac Cream Soup

Heat a stick of butter until it sizzles, then add a half pint of goose livers. Dust with salt, black pepper, paprika, thyme, minced garlic, and parsley. Fry quickly on both sides, then flambé with a half cup of fine cognac. Set aside until livers cool, then chop them into bite-sized bits, reserving the pan drippings. Meanwhile, combine in a soup pot a quart of light cream with a cup of diced potatoes, a half cup of chopped shallots, a half cup of flour, four tablespoons of chicken bouillon, two tablespoons of chopped chives, and a teaspoon of tarragon. Simmer until the potatoes are soft, then blend until smooth. Add a dash of nutmeg and the chopped goose livers and drippings. Simmer fifteen minutes and serve.

Cream of Wild Rice Soup

Boil one cup of wild rice in three cups of white wine, covered, for about thirty minutes. Then add a half cup of thin-sliced leeks, two tablespoons of beef bouillon, and one quart of light cream. Blend two cups of this mixture until smooth and return it to the pot. Season to taste with black pepper, thyme, and salt.

CLEAR SOUPS

People used to keep stock always simmering on the back of the stove. Bones, left over from God only knows what, were thrown into a large pot along with a couple of carrots and onions and a generous quantity of herbs. From this stock would be made clear broths, consommes, and sauce bases. The Shakers used to feed one specialty, a veal and barley broth that was later found to be filled with potassium and magnesium, to patients in the infirmary. Soup has yet to lose its reputation as one of the best medicines around.

I remember when my grandmother used to buy just the feet of the chicken for her stock, but the advent of pesticides, which chickens must scratch around in, put a lid on that soup permanently.

When you buy chicken breasts today, choose the ones with the bone and skin on. Remove the bone and skin yourself and collect them in a bag in the freezer. It won't be long before you can boil up a big pot of chicken stock (just simmer the bones and skin with water and salt), and it will cost you almost nothing. I needn't elaborate on the health benefits of chicken soup. Just walk into any Hadassah meeting and announce that you don't feel well—I guarantee you will hear all about it.

The claret in the following recipe is to the soup as the egg is to a New York chocolate egg cream (remember those?). No claret, no egg.

Chicken Claret with Casaba Melon

Bring to a boil four cups of chicken stock (or, if you must, four cups of water plus four tablespoons chicken bouillon), with one cup of dry white wine, a quarter cup each of white vermouth and dry sherry, a half cup of thin-sliced shallots, and a half teaspoon each of black pepper, curry powder, mace, marjoram, and thyme. Simmer until the shallots soften. Add the chopped flesh of one casaba melon and serve.

Once you have a supply of chicken broth, Chicken Claret with Casaba Melon is not the only direction you can go. Another is the Oriental route—add chopped cucumber and sprinkle crunched *nori* (seaweed) across the top. You could also throw in some Chinese string noodles, dash with soy sauce, and add garlic. Or try adding chopped lettuce, shredded summer squash, and chopped fresh tomatoes. The idea is to choose inexpensive ingredients that will cook within minutes in hot broth to make a healthful and non-fattening dish. What more can you ask of chicken soup? Seafood is another good ingredient on which to base a clear soup. The following three recipes do not require any premade stock.

One-Pot Fish Soup

In a large soup pot heat four tablespoons of olive oil. Slice four ripe red tomatoes and a green pepper into the hot oil, and shave in a carrot with a potato peeler. Add six chopped garlic cloves, a chopped medium onion, and a tablespoon each of saffron and fresh-ground black pepper. Sauté this mixture until it thickens, then stir in a cup each of dry sherry and white wine and two cups of clam broth. Add one pound of bay scallops, a half pound of fresh crabmeat, six fresh clams, six fresh mussels, a two-pound lobster (quartered while still live—no problem for a real man), a half cup of grated Parmesan, and salt to taste. Cover and simmer until the lobster turns red and its meat is tender to the touch. Serve as is or ladle over curried rice.

Seafood in a Sherried Clam Broth

Combine in a soup pot: a cup of clam juice, four ounces of scallops, a half pint of oysters, twelve ounces of langostinos (one package), a thin-sliced leek, one cup of dry sherry, four cups of water, a teaspoon of black pepper, a teaspoon of saffron, salt to taste, a half cup of chopped lettuce, two thin-sliced carrots, and one chopped pimiento. Simmer until the leeks are soft. Serve.

Into a soup pot put one quart of Clamato juice, one cup of dry sherry, a cup of fine-sliced onion, a carrot shredded with a potato peeler, one tablespoon of minced garlic, one-quarter cup of frozen orange concentrate, a half tablespoon of chili powder, and one pound of raw shelled and deveined shrimp. Sprinkle with salt and pepper and bring to a boil. Add three leaves of *nori* (Japanese seaweed), broken into small pieces. Serve as soon as the shrimps are cooked. The total cooking time for this soup should be about 10 minutes.

Tomato Clam Broth with Shrimp and Nori

Everything in this book, and in my first cookbook too, you should have learned when you were a kid, helping to throw the bones in the stock pot as soon as you were big enough to reach. A kid's knowledge of soup should not be limited to opening a can. It amazes me how little so many children are learning from their parents about working, feeding themselves and all those other basics like sewing on a button and getting the wash white. In contrast, my godson's father taught him, at age three, what fun it is to work as they both repaired a chair. He introduced work into his child's life as a wonderful thing to look forward to. And his mother feeds him and his baby sister pure, fresh food. She knows nutrition and plans the meals accordingly. It's lovely how relative everything is. Put a lot of wonderful things into a stock pot, and you'll have a wonderful soup. Put a lot of wonderful things into a child's mind, and you'll have a wonderful adult. The universe is to you exactly what you are to it. I'm talking cooking here!

Salads and Dressings

One of the many laudable things about California is its abundance of green grocers with their always incredible selections. I am delighted that supermarkets in the East are beginning to follow the lead. The introduction of salad bars in supermarkets and hamburger and pizza joints is an obvious sign that Americans all over the country are trying to eat better. Now they just need to venture beyond iceberg, cottage cheese, and canned peaches.

People are becoming more and more aware of the "F factor," the "fiber" in their diets. I'm told that a few lettuce leaves provide you with about three percent of the fiber you need daily to maintain your plumbing. So salads are a great place to start if you need to increase your fiber intake. But you needn't set up a salad bar like the ones in the pizza joints—salad is anything cold tossed together in a bowl and served with a dressing.

Any wonderful concoction of thin-sliced or shredded fresh fruits or vegetables (or both) works. For instance: carrots, turnips,

Jerusalem artichokes, dandelion greens, and fiddlehead ferns with lots of snipped parsley, dill, and basil. Served with a dressing of honey and lemon juice, it's a salad that curbs your appetite and fills you with fiber, vitamins, and minerals.

When creating a salad, remember to include things orange and dark green. And don't forget the leftovers from last night's dinner— add a can of tuna and you've something vaguely "Nicoise."

Zucchini and Grapefruit in Raspberry–Honey Dressing

Shred enough zucchini to fill three to four cups and spread it across a bed of romaine or Bibb lettuce. Peel a grapefruit and arrange thin slices (not sections) of the fruit around the zucchini. Spoon with Raspberry-Honey Dressing.

Raspberry-Honey Dressing: Combine one cup of oil and one-third cup of Raspberry-Champagne Vinegar (page 35). Blend in a half cup of raspberry preserves and two tablespoons each of honey and a good mustard.

Sweet and Sour Apples, Bacon, and Zucchini Salad

Thin-slice two large apples and two zucchini into a salad bowl. Chop a half pound of bacon, then fry it until crisp. To the pan of bacon add salt, black pepper, a handful of chopped parsley, a sprinkle each of fresh basil and rosemary, a half cup of brown sugar, a quarter cup of vinegar, and the juice of two lemons. Cook the mixture until it sizzles, then pour it over the apples and zucchini. Toss and serve.

Apple, Pineapple, and Cucumber Salad

This salad makes its own dressing. Toss together the thin-sliced fruit of one pineapple, two red apples, and one good-sized cucumber in a salad bowl. Refrigerate about thirty minutes so that the juices can mingle, then serve on a bed of lettuce.

Pineapple and Red Cabbage Salad

This colorful duo is great for a low-calorie diet. Simply grate equal amounts of red cabbage and fresh pineapple. Serve on lettuce.

Shredded White Radish and Sliced Orange

Shred enough white radishes to fill three to four cups. Peel two seedless oranges and slice them as thin as possible. Fan the orange slices across a bed of lettuce, mound the shredded radish over them, and bathe with Lemon-Pepper Dressing.

Lemon-Pepper Dressing: Combine three-fourths cup of oil, one-third cup of Lemon-Pepper Vinegar (page 36), and two tablespoons of brown sugar. Add salt, black pepper, and dill to taste.

Cucumbers and Strawberries with Strawberry–Port Wine Vinegar

Peel cucumbers and slice them thin; combine them in a salad bowl with an equal volume of sliced strawberries. Toss with oil of your choice, then sprinkle with Strawbery–Port Wine Vinegar (page 35) and drizzle with honey.

Peaches and Sliced Radishes

Slice a bunch of radishes and two good-sized unpeeled peaches. Lightly toss them together with a half cup of oil of your choice, a third cup of Orange–Juniper Berry Vinegar (page 35), and a half cup of maple syrup.

Bacon, Yogurt, and Chives on Peaches and Crab Legs

Fan thin slices of peach across a bed of lettuce. Lay a crab leg between every two slices of fruit. Dress with two cups of yogurt into which you've mixed a half pound of crumbled cooked bacon, a half cup of chopped chives, and salt, black pepper, and minced garlic to taste.

Mangoes and Smoked Salmon

Peel and slice mangoes. Arrange the mango slices on a lettuce leaf, alternating them with thin slices of smoked salmon. Sprinkle with fresh lime or orange juice.

Cut the rind from a cranshaw melon. Slice the melon and arrange the pieces with alternating slivers of cold, raw salmon. Shake one-quarter cup each of olive oil and soy sauce with one teaspoon each of ground ginger, lemon juice, and lime juice. When the dressing is well blended, pour it over the fish and fruit.

Melon with Raw Salmon in a Ginger Sauce

Wash and trim one pound of spinach. Drain it well and set it aside in a large salad bowl. Dice a half pound of bacon and fry it until crisp. Put the bacon and drippings into a blender and add a quarter cup of vinegar, the juice of one lemon, a one-minute egg, a tablespoon of chopped garlic, some black pepper, and two tablespoons each of prepared mustard, catsup, and tamari sauce. Blend until smooth. Return this sauce to the pan and heat until sizzling. Add four tablespoons of cognac and ignite immediately. Pour the flaming sauce over the spinach, throw in a handful of grated Parmesan, and toss thirty-two times. (Kitchen legend has it that thirty-two tosses will give you a perfectly dressed salad.)

Spinach and Bacon Cognac Caesar

Pick a couple of handfuls of the youngest, most tender-looking dandelion greens you can find. (Who doesn't have dandelions sharing space with the lawn?) Wash and dry them, and toss them into a bowl. Shake together a little less than a cup of oil, a quarter cup of Sherry–Black Walnut Vinegar (page 35), a quarter cup of brown sugar, a sliced small onion, and salt and black pepper to taste. Dress the greens with this mixture and garnish with sliced hard-cooked eggs.

Dandelion Greens with Black Walnut Dressing

Emerald City Salad

Start with equal amounts of several different greens—romaine, Bibb, leaf lettuce, escarole, spinach, perhaps even shredded green cabbage. Add a chopped cucumber, several peeled and thin-sliced kiwi fruits, a handful of chopped celery, a handful of mixed chopped chives and scallions, and a couple of spoonfuls each of marjoram, basil, and tarragon. Toss well with Emerald City Dressing and serve.

Emerald City Dressing: Start with a cup of oil of your choice. Add a quarter cup of white wine vinegar and a quarter cup of Rose's Lime Juice. Whisk in a quarter cup of honey and two tablespoons each of prepared mustard and chopped garlic. Season to taste with black pepper.

Nasturtium Salad

Chop a head of Bibb lettuce, or another type of lettuce if you prefer. Add a couple of handfuls of nasturtium blossoms and sprinkle the flower and lettuce mixture with oil, white wine vinegar, salt, and black pepper. The dressing should be light so as not to detract from the taste of these delicate flowers.

VINEGARS, OILS, AND DRESSINGS

Not long ago, while I was browsing through one of those wonderful shops that carry those wonderful foods that are always too wonderfully expensive, I came across a bottle of raspberry vinegar priced at eight dollars and fifty cents. I figured that by the time I bought a liter of olive oil for another twelve dollars and a jar of mustard for seven, I'd probably have to take out a loan to buy the lettuce. The idea of making my own vinegars and oils began to intrigue me. And since it's such an easy and inexpensive thing to do, I thought I would pass the information along. Not only is a homemade condiment elegant in your own cooking, but it also makes one of the best gifts for any occasion. Two things you will need to make your own vinegars are vinegar extract (a good one from Germany is usually available at specialty food shops) and fruit extracts (some are artificial; try to find the natural ones). You will also need fresh fruit and a selection of liquids. For instance, you could make a strawberry–port wine vinegar, a strawberry–champagne vinegar, or a plain strawberry vinegar. To the basic mixture you could add a variety of things. How about a strawberry-pepper-port wine vinegar or a strawberry-cucumber-champagne vinegar? Following are a couple of intriguing combinations that have worked well for me. I suggest that you let these mixtures stand for thirty days before you use them, although I have been known to use them the day I make them, and the results have been just fine.

Strawberry–Port Wine Vinegar

Combine one cup of vinegar extract, two cups of port wine, and one and a half ounces of strawberry extract. Fill a sterilized quart jar with hulled strawberries, then pour in the flavored vinegar. Add more wine to fill the jar, then seal.

Sherry–Black Walnut Vinegar

Combine one cup of vinegar extract, two cups of Burgundy wine, and one and a half ounces of black walnut extract. Fill a sterilized quart jar with unpitted black cherries, then pour in the flavored vinegar. Add more wine to fill the jar, then seal.

Raspberry–Champagne Vinegar

Pour two cups of champagne, one cup of vinegar extract, and one and a half ounces of raspberry extract in a sterilized quart jar filled with raspberries. If necessary, add more champagne to fill the jar.

Orange–Juniper Berry Vinegar

Slice one small unpeeled orange into a sterilized quart jar; add two or three bay leaves and one tablespoon of juniper berries. Combine one cup of vinegar extract and two cups of dry white wine with a quarter

(Orange–Juniper Berry Vinegar) ounce of orange oil. Pour this mixture over the other ingredients and add enough wine to fill the jar.

Lemon-Pepper Vinegar In a sterilized quart jar combine one cup of vinegar extract, two cups of sweet white wine, four tablespoons of green peppercorns, the juice of two lemons, and two thin slices of lemon.

Almond-Sherry Vinegar Place a cup of almonds in a sterilized quart jar. Add one cup of vinegar extract, an ounce and a half of almond extract, and enough cream or dry sherry to fill the jar.

Don't hesitate to combine your favorite fruits, wines, liqueurs, nuts, herbs, and spices in ways that strike your fancy. And don't neglect the potential health benefits of some such concoctions. Once again, what I have given you is really just an outline—take the initiative and create a vinegar uniquely your own. Peaches, limes, sour cherries, and blueberries with May wine and green peppercorns could be lovely. Once you're accustomed to looking at such vivacious vinegars, of course, the other half of your cruet set will seem depressingly mediocre—but only until you master the process of making flavored oils.

It's simple. Just put some herbs or flavoring in a bottle and pour in the oil. The oil will preserve your fresh garden herbs and other additions. It's almost silly to give you precise measurements for the oil or even to specify what kinds to use. I like pure olive oil best; it seems to have more body and tastes far better than any corn oil, safflower oil, soy oil, or blend. But it's all a matter of personal preference.

Flavored oils are a joy to use not only in salads, but in everyday cooking as well. Fresh salmon sautéed in a black walnut oil is terrific, as is shredded zucchini sautéed in dandelion oil and chicken fried in savory oil.

Nut-flavored oils are a good place to start. Grind a half cup of walnuts with a cup of oil, pour the mixture into a quart bottle, and fill the bottle the rest of the way with oil. In a week or two you will have walnut-flavored oil, which you can decant as you use it.

Now you have the basics for a salad that would make any "best-dressed" list. "Oil and vinegar" will never have the same meaning for you. Here are a few other salad dressings of which I am very fond.

Curried Maple Syrup Dressing

Add one-third cup of vinegar to one and a half cups of oil. Blend in a half cup of chopped onion, a quarter cup of Dijon mustard, two tablespoons of curry powder, and the juice of one lemon. Season with salt and black pepper, and sweeten with a half cup or more of maple syrup.

Strawberry and Honey Dressing

Combine in a blender a cup of oil, two cups of sliced fresh strawberries, a quarter cup each of honey and white wine vinegar, two tablespoons of prepared mustard, and one teaspoon each of cinnamon and black pepper.

Black Olive and Sour Cream Dressing

Whir in a blender one six-ounce can of pitted black olives, three-fourths cup of oil, one-fourth cup of red wine vinegar, one-fourth cup of hot mustard, a handful of chopped parsley, a tablespoon of chopped garlic, and salt and black pepper to taste. Blend until almost smooth, then fold the mixture into a pint of sour cream.

Pimiento and Sour Cream Dressing

In a blender mix three-fourths cup of oil, one-fourth cup of white wine vinegar, three tablespoons of Dijon mustard, the juice of one lemon, two canned pimientos (with their juice), one pint of sour cream, and salt and white pepper to taste. When smooth, pour on any salad or cold vegetable.

Fish

When I was growing up in Chicago we could afford two kinds of fish, canned tuna and frozen halibut. My mother fixed tuna casseroles in as many different ways as the Kraft Music Hall suggested. Remember that announcer with the deep voice? "Fill the bottom of your casserole dish with crushed potato chips; add well-cooked noodles, a can of mushroom soup, two cans of tuna; cover with generous slices of Velveeta cheese; and top it all off with a thick layer of Miracle Whip. Ummm, doesn't that sound good?" We had Tuna Surprise, Tuna Magic, Tuna à la King, and, of course, Tuna Wiggle! To this day, I cannot pass the tuna aisle in the supermarket without getting the old urge to run away from home. Here are a few ideas that may keep you from leaving home.

Tuna Steaks in Olive Oil and Honey

Ask your fishmonger to slice you some tuna steaks about half an inch thick. Cover the bottom of a skillet with olive oil, and heat the oil until it almost begins to smoke. Lay the tuna steaks in the smouldering oil. Season both sides with salt, black pepper, and garlic as the steaks cook. Once they are browned on both sides, brush on this mixture: four tablespoons of honey, two tablespoons each of soy sauce and catsup, one tablespoon of vinegar, and the juice of one lemon. Glaze both sides, turning often, as the fish continues to cook. Sprinkle with fresh parsley when nearly done.

A thick cut of any oily fish can be used in place of fresh tuna in the following recipe. Swordfish, shark, and sturgeon are all excellent substitutes.

(Tuna Steaks in Olive Oil and Honey)

Ask your fishmonger to cut you a thick piece of tuna this time, three or more inches wide. Rub this "roast" with melted butter, salt, black pepper, garlic, and lemon juice. In an ovenproof pan, brown the fish on all sides in hot oil; remove from the pan and set aside. Lightly sauté four cups of chopped beet greens in the pan juices, and then stir in a cup of dry white wine. Lay the tuna roast atop the bed of greens, and alternate thin slices of tomato, onion, and cucumber across the top. Season with salt, black pepper, tarragon, and lemon juice; cover tightly. Bake at 400° for an hour to an hour and fifteen minutes. Slice into serving pieces and spoon the greens and juices over.

Tuna Roast in Beet Greens

Slice haddock fillets into pieces three to four inches wide, and toss the pieces quickly in hot olive oil. Season with salt, black pepper, garlic, and parsley, and brown about three to four minutes on each side. Remove the fish pieces from the skillet and set aside. Slice six ripe plums into the pan juices. Season with a quarter cup of chopped scallions, a quarter cup of brandy, some ginger, and a sprinkling of brown sugar or a drizzle of honey. Push this mixture to the sides

Haddock in Plums and Brandy

(Haddock in Plums and Brandy)

of the pan, and add the fish. Spoon the fruit mixture over the fish pieces, and simmer for six to eight minutes.

Haddock with Langostinos in a White Wine–Parsley Sauce

Butter a three- to four-pound haddock fillet, lay it in a baking dish, and bake it uncovered at 500° for twelve to fifteen minutes. Drain the juices, and reserve them for the sauce. Pour the White Wine–Parsley Sauce over the haddock, and bake for another seven to eight minutes.

White Wine–Parsley Sauce: Mix four tablespoons of flour into the same amount of melted butter; gradually add a cup of white wine, a cup of chopped fresh parsley, and the juices from the cooked haddock. Blend well, then simmer five minutes. Fold in one pound of langostinos and ladle over haddock.

Striped bass is an oily fish. The oil sits close to the skin, so you might wish to skin the fish. But unless you are really put off by the taste, you might as well leave the skin on—it's a healthy addition to your diet.

Striped Bass in a Cognac–Sour Cream Sauce with Scallops

Cut bass steaks or fillets in slices three-fourths to one inch thick. Dip the slices in beaten egg and then in flour and place them in a pan with four or five tablespoons of sizzling butter. Sprinkle with salt and pepper to taste, and add a good handful of chopped parsley. Fry until the fish is lightly browned on both sides, then lay it in a baking dish. In the same pan sauté one and a half pounds of washed and drained scallops (bay scallops are preferable, but others will work—you might slice large ones). Season them while they are cooking with salt and pepper, and sprinkle with a quarter cup of flour, the juice of one lemon, and a good hit of cognac. Stir well so the scallops don't stick to the bottom of the pan. Add two cups of sour cream and more salt and pepper if needed. When well combined, pour the sauce over the bass in the baking dish. Bake uncovered at 425° for fifteen to twenty minutes.

(Striped Bass in a Cognac–Sour Cream Sauce with Scallops)

Striped Bass with Crabmeat in Cucumber Sauce

Prepare bass as described in the preceding recipe, or just lay the raw pieces in a baking dish, season with salt and pepper and lemon juice, and bake uncovered at 500° for twelve to fifteen minutes.

After cooking the bass by either method, add the prepared crabmeat, cover, and bake at 500° for ten minutes. Remove the baked crabmeat and bass, stir any pan drippings or juices into the sauce, and ladle the sauce over. Serve.

Crabmeat: Into one pound of fresh crabmeat mix four tablespoons of melted butter, a good tablespoon of chopped garlic, one egg, the juice of one lime, and a little salt and black pepper.

Sauce: Melt four tablespoons of butter in a saucepan until it sizzles. Add one diced medium cucumber, four tablespoons of flour, some salt and black pepper, and a touch of dill or tarragon (or both). Stir well, then gradually add one cup of dry white wine. Simmer fifteen minutes.

Crab-stuffed Sole in Tomato-Cognac Sauce

Butter one side of sole fillets, then cover them with crabmeat. Sprinkle with salt, black pepper, and lemon juice. Roll up the fillets carefully, cut them in half, and lay them in a baking dish with the cut sides facing up. Pour plenty of sauce over the stuffed fish and bake uncovered at 500° for about twelve minutes.

Sauce: Chop a couple of tomatoes into four tablespoons of melted butter; add garlic, salt, black pepper, basil, and lemon. Sauté until the tomatoes are almost reduced to a paste. Remove from heat, splash with cognac, and pour over fish.

Fillet of Sole with Mussels in Sherry Butter

Steam three to four pounds of cleaned mussels just long enough to open, about one minute, and discard any that remain tightly closed. Or start with two cups (about a pound) of already shucked mussels.

Lay about three pounds of sole fillets in a bake-and-serve dish and cover with the shucked mussels. Baste generously with a mixture of a half cup each of dry sherry and hot melted butter, seasoned with salt, black pepper, garlic, and parsley. Bake at 500° for about twelve minutes.

Fillet of Sole in Duxelle Cream

Lay about three pounds of sole fillets in a bake-and-serve dish. Sprinkle them with salt and black pepper to taste. Mix half a cup of duxelles (page 12) with a cup of heavy cream, some salt and black pepper, a good handful of chopped parsley, and a little ground nutmeg. Pour this mixture over the sole and bake at 500° for twelve minutes.

Salmon with Artichoke in Orange-Lobster Cream

Butter a large baking dish and lay a whole side (about four to five pounds) of boned and skinned Atlantic salmon in the center. Surround with thin slices of unpeeled orange, and lay an artichoke heart atop each fruit slice. Sprinkle with salt, black pepper, garlic, and lemon juice. Bake at 500° for twelve to fifteen minutes. Remove from oven, ladle with Orange–Lobster Cream Sauce, and serve.

Orange-Lobster Cream Sauce: Melt a half cup of butter in a saucepan, then stir in two to three tablespoons of flour. Add one and a half cups of light cream, a half cup of sour cream, one-fourth cup of frozen orange concentrate, one tablespoon each of chopped garlic and summer savory, and salt and black pepper to taste. Simmer for fifteen minutes, stirring often. Pour into a blender, add an egg, and whirl until smooth. Return to the saucepan, and fold in one pound of chopped, cooked lobster meat. Simmer another ten minutes before serving.

(Salmon with Artichoke in Orange-Lobster Cream)

Cut salmon into inch-thick steaks. Place the slices on a buttered cookie sheet and sprinkle lightly with salt, black pepper, parsley, and lime juice. Bake uncovered at 400° for twelve to fifteen minutes. Arrange the salmon on a serving dish; let cool. Prepare the custard cream sauce.

Orange Custard Cream: Combine thoroughly in a blender: four eggs, a cup of melted butter, the juice of one lemon, some white pepper, and a tablespoon each of frozen orange concentrate and chicken bouillon. Pour into a saucepan and slowly heat, stirring until the mixture thickens to the consistency of pudding. If the mixture is lumpy, return it to the blender and whirl until smooth. Serve chilled in a sauceboat with the cold salmon.

Cold Salmon in an Orange Custard Cream

Cut a pound of lobster meat into pieces of equal size, and divide the pieces evenly among clean scallop shells. Set two artichoke hearts on each shell. Cover with heavy cream and season with salt, black pepper, and minced garlic. Sprinkle with chopped parsley and bake at 500° for about ten minutes.

Creamed Lobster with Artichoke Hearts

Chop about a pound of cooked lobster meat and place in a bowl. Add one thin-sliced medium onion, a half pound of crumbled crisp-fried bacon, a half cup of chopped scallions, and two sliced (not sectioned) oranges. Stir in one cup of sour cream, a quarter cup

Lobster-Orange Salad in Sambuca and Bacon Sour Cream

of **Sambuca**, the juice of one lemon, and salt and black pepper to taste. Combine thoroughly. Serve on thin slices of melon or on lettuce leaves.

Cold Smoked Mussels with Sauerkraut

To one pint of cold smoked mussels add a pint of sour cream, a half cup of thin-sliced onions, a quarter cup each of sauerkraut and red wine, and two table-spoons of brown sugar. Season with salt and black pepper. Serve on a bed of lettuce with thin orange slices.

Frogs' Legs in Lemon and Pimiento-Pernod Sauce

Lay about twenty pairs of thawed frogs' legs in a bake-and-serve dish. Cover with sauce and bake, covered, at 400° for thirty minutes.

Sauce: Combine in a blender two pimientos with a quarter cup of Pernod, a quarter cup of melted butter, one and a quarter cups of white wine, the juice of one lemon, and a sprinkling of salt and black pepper. Blend till smooth.

SUSHI

The most important thing to remember about Sushi is that it's nothing more than Japanese stuffed cabbage. The only difference is that instead of cabbage they use seaweed, and instead of ground beef and rice they use raw fish and rice. It's that simple.

Prepare some white rice, boiling it without adding butter or salt. Toss it while still warm with vinegar, about two tablespoons to four cups of rice. Tossing helps the air to circulate around the grains of rice so that it doesn't get sticky. The rice should hold together however. Set the rice aside momentarily while you prepare the seaweed, called *nori*, which comes in sheets that look like dark green cellophane. Toast a sheet lightly and quickly over an open flame; either a gas stove or candle will work. Then lay the sheet flat in front of you.

Spoon out an inch-wide strip of rice parallel to and about an inch away from the lengthwise edge of the sheet of *nori*. Place a length of raw fish beside the rice. Add some pickled ginger and perhaps some red caviar, and roll up the *nori* as you would a cigarette. Moistening the last inch or so of the *nori* will seal it. Slice the sushi in inch-thick disks and serve with soy sauce, mustard sauce, or a sweet and sour sauce.

You might try making sushi with lightly cooked corn, cream cheese, or wild rice instead of using white rice. If you're not fond of raw fish or are afraid to try it, use cooked lobster meat, crabmeat, or smoked salmon. Sometimes I make it with cream cheese and smoked salmon, "Jewpanese" style. Add cucumber sticks, bean sprouts, or slivered scallions instead of, or in addition to, the fish. Or use leftover turkey, ham, or chicken. It's probably no longer sushi from a purist's viewpoint, but unless you're a purist (which is doubtful if you've gotten this far into this book), what do you care?

Birds

Birds and fish seem to go really well together. At least *I* like the combination—this will be evident in the selection of recipes in this chapter. I have some favorite favorites in the bird-and-fish category that you also might enjoy.

The first recipe serves only four; it would be expensive to prepare for more since it calls for lobster tails. You can buy four whole lobsters and retrieve the tails yourself, or you can buy just a pound of shelled lobster meat. If you do the latter, ask the fishmonger to cook the lobster only slightly, just enough so the meat can be removed from the shell. (This is important because lobster tends to toughen with prolonged cooking, and for this recipe it will have to cook again.) A pound of shelled lobster should give you about four tails and lots of claw meat. And God only knows how much guilt you'll save yourself by not having to throw half a dozen living things into boiling water.

CHICKEN

Start by boning and skinning four small chicken breasts (freeze the bones and skin for soup). Fry the breasts in four tablespoons of sizzling butter until browned on both sides. Season with a half cup of chopped parsley, two tablespoons of minced garlic, the juice of one lemon, paprika, salt, and black pepper. Pour in three-fourths cup of dry sherry (Amontillado would be perfect). Cook the breasts another couple of minutes on each side, then arrange them in a bake-and-serve dish. Drain the skillet juices into a blender and add two cups of light cream, four tablespoons of flour, two tablespoons of lobster base (if you like), and a sprinkling of white pepper. Blend until smooth, then pour the sauce into the skillet and simmer until it thickens. Split four lobster tails down the center and fan one across each chicken breast. Pour some sauce over each portion and top with a total of two cups of grated Havarti cheese. Bake at 400° for about twenty minutes.

Sherried Chicken Breast with Lobster Tails and Cheese

Pound one large boned chicken breast as thin as possible (to prevent the chicken from flying around the room while you do this, lay the breast between a couple of thicknesses of foil). Cover the flattened breast with a generous layer of Beet Green Pesto (page 83) or the pesto of your choice. Roll the breast lengthwise, and slice into portions about an inch thick. Lay these cut side up on a cookie sheet. Cover each piece of breast with a thin slice of Brie and bake at 450° for about twenty minutes. Serve.

Chicken Breast with Beet Green Pesto and Brie

Chicken Stir-Fry with Raisins and Sambuca Mayonnaise

To serve six, flatten and quarter three chicken breasts. Toss the pieces into four tablespoons of hot olive oil in a skillet or wok. Add a cup of raisins, half a cup of chopped scallions, and a quarter cup of white wine. Stir-fry until the chicken is done. Scoop into a serving dish, stir in Hot Sambuca Mayonnaise, and serve.

Hot Sambuca Mayonnaise: Start with homemade mayonnaise or buy one that's all-natural. Combine one cup of mayonnaise with a quarter cup of minced scallions, one egg yolk, the juice of one lemon, four tablespoons of Sambuca, one tablespoon of olive oil, one teaspoon of tarragon, and black pepper to taste. Blend thoroughly, then heat slowly in a saucepan until the mixture thickens. If it separates, whirl in a blender.

Sweet and Sour Chicken Breast with Mussels

For six people, flatten three good-sized breasts, halve them, and quickly brown them on both sides in four tablespoons of bubbling bacon fat. Season with salt, black pepper, garlic, and chopped fresh parsley. Add three cups of shelled raw mussels, four tablespoons of vinegar, the juice of one lemon, and four to eight tablespoons of honey. Cover and simmer for three minutes. Serve with a wonderful salad of sliced tomatoes in gingered lime juice.

If mussels are not easily available, you might use oysters, lobsters, or scallops. You could also replace the mussels with crisp bacon, ham slices, or smoked salmon. Or you could make it an all-fish dish and use salmon, swordfish, or haddock instead of chicken. Vegetarians could use sesame oil in place of bacon grease, eggplant (or sliced tomatoes or zucchini) in place of chicken, and chestnuts or grapes instead of mussels. Recipes aren't sacred—shape them to your tastes and inclinations.

DUCK

It is now possible to buy what is known as "breast of duck." I think that a good part of it is actually back, though it does not include any leg. Less trouble than a whole duck, these breasts are perfect for roasting. And if you don't let yourself wonder what became of the rest of the bird, it's a fun meat to eat.

Breast of Duck in Blueberries and Crème de Cassis

Lay duck breasts (one per person) on a raised rack in a roasting pan. (If you line the pan with foil, you'll have less to clean afterwards.) Season with salt, black pepper, and coriander. Bake at 500° for forty to sixty minutes, or until the skin is browned and crispy. Remove the duck from the oven and drain off the grease. Lower the oven temperature to 400° and roast another twenty to thirty minutes, basting at least twice with Blueberries and Creme de Cassis Sauce.

Blueberries and Creme de Cassis Sauce: While the duck is baking, whip one cup of blueberry jam and two cups of creme de cassis in a blender with a half stick of butter and a half cup of your choice of mustard. Simmer this mixture about thirty minutes, then gently stir in a pint of fresh blueberries and simmer for fifteen minutes more. Use for basting the duck.

Breast of Duck in Cranberries and Crème de Cassis

Follow the directions for baked breast of duck in the preceding recipe, but season the breasts with cardamon instead of coriander and baste with cranberry sauce prepared as follows.

Sauce: Heat in a saucepan two cups of creme de cassis with two cups of maple syrup or honey, two sticks of butter, one-half cup of frozen orange concentrate, four cups of fresh cranberries, and one tablespoon each of salt, black pepper, and minced garlic. Simmer until the cranberries soften.

**Breast of Duck
in Rhubarb
and Crème de Cassis**

Prepare breast of duck as directed in the first recipe, using rhubarb in the basting sauce this time.

Sauce: Grate two cups of rhubarb into a saucepan. Add two cups of creme de cassis; one cup each of brandy, maple syrup, and butter; and one-half cup each of mustard, honey, and frozen orange concentrate. Bring to a boil, then simmer until reduced by a third.

**Breast of Duck
in Grape Leaves
with Grapefruit**

Season six duck breasts with salt, black pepper, and cardamon. Roast on a raised rack set into a pan for forty-five to sixty minutes in a 500° oven. Cool breasts enough to handle, then slice the meat off the bone and cut it into thin strips. Peel and section three seedless grapefruit. Lay some duck meat and fruit on each grape leaf; you will probably use twelve to sixteen. Sprinkle each portion with garlic, nutmeg, ginger, and a tablespoon of minced scallion. Fold three edges of the leaf over the stuffing and roll it tightly. Arrange in an oiled bake-and-serve dish. Mix the juice from another grapefruit with equal parts of soy sauce and honey; drizzle this sauce over the stuffed grape leaves, and bake for about fifteen minutes in a 500° oven.

For preparing Duck Breast in Grape Leaves with Grapefruit, you can buy a jar of perfectly matched grape leaves in just about any supermarket. You could also use collards, kale, or cauliflower leaves. You could even wrap your own bird-and-fruit combination in lettuce or *nori*—this is beginning to sound like sushi (pages 44-45)!

**Hot Mangoes
Stuffed with Duck**

Cook and debone duck breasts as suggested in the preceding recipe, but use cardamon instead of coriander for seasoning. Peel, seed, and halve as many mangoes as you'll need, figuring one half per person. Scoop out the center (save it for the filling) to make room for the duck. Quickly sauté the duck strips in a half cup of butter. Stir in the reserved mango, the juice of one lemon, two tablespoons of mustard, one tablespoon of honey, and some salt and pepper. Divide this mixture among the mango halves and arrange them in a bake-and-serve dish. Bake for fifteen minutes in a 500° oven. Serve with a flaming sherry butter.

(Hot Mangoes Stuffed with Duck)

QUAIL

Nobody wants to order them. I'm not surprised. The kind that are available have nothing in common with the wild variety, the real thing. A wild bird that feeds on berries bears no relation to what you buy in the market—frozen, half-boned (twelve to a cardboard box), and tasting a little too much like dark chicken meat. Yet, I suppose if someone asked you to dine on "Brace of Quail Stuffed with Walnut Cheese and Smoked Mussels in a Champagne and Lobster Pâté Cream Sauce," you'd really give it second thoughts before turning it down. Taking what we have and making it as wonderful as possible only opens the door to our own potential, which, as we all know, is limitless.

Two quails per person is ample; this recipe serves six. Butter the insides of twelve birds and dust the whole bird with salt and pepper. Combine, in a food processor or by hand, eight ounces each of cream cheese and grated Havarti, two tablespoons of chopped walnuts, and one teaspoon white pepper. When the mixture is smoothly blended, fold in half a pound of smoked mussels. Stuff the quail and butter the outside of each bird—nasturtium butter (page 7) would be lovely at this point. Set in a baking dish, splash with a cup of white wine, and bake uncovered

Quail with Walnut Cheese and Smoked Mussels in a Champagne and Lobster Sauce

(Quail with Walnut Cheese and Smoked Mussels in a Champagne and Lobster Sauce)

in a preheated 500° oven for fifteen minutes. Cover, then cook ten more minutes. Ladle with sauce and serve.

Champagne and Lobster Pâté Cream Sauce: Using the chopper blade in your food processor, blend one pound of fresh-cooked lobster meat with a stick of butter, an egg, a teaspoon chopped garlic, the juice of one lemon, a sprinkling of nutmeg and black pepper, and one tablespoon each of heavy cream, fine cognac, chopped scallions, chopped parsley, and lobster base (optional). Process only until well blended, but not yet a paste. Transfer to a saucepan, add half a cup of dry champagne and one cup each of heavy and light cream. Simmer until sauce thickens.

Naturally the critic will say, "It's easy to make the ordinary wonderful when you have unlimited funds for the ornaments." And naturally I would agree. But the basis for my philosophy is that extravagance has nothing to do with cost and everything to do with imagination. It could just as easily have been, "Brace of Quails Stuffed with Almonds and Pears in a Rose Petal Cream Sauce." I won't give that recipe here so that the "critic" might have the chance to explore his own potential—and see just how unlimited it is.

Boned Quail in a Crown of Lobster Pâté

Prepare the lobster pâté as suggested in the preceding recipe, but process it until it definitely becomes a paste. Dust twelve semi-boned quail (you can usually buy them just that way) with flour and fry, six minutes on each side, in butter. Set cooked quail in a baking dish and spoon lobster paste into a pastry tube with a large "border" tip. Decorate the dish of quails with lobster pâté and set an artichoke heart in the center. Bake at 500° for about twelve minutes, top with a dollop of thick hollandaise, and serve.

Dip twelve semi-boned quail in flour. Fry in a half cup of butter, sprinkling with salt, pepper, garlic, and parsley. The birds will take about six minutes on each side. Remove to a bake-and-serve dish. In the same pan, fry one pound of goose livers with one cup of chopped mushrooms. Season with a tablespoon of thyme; add salt, pepper, and garlic to taste. When the livers have browned on both sides, flambé the mixture with a quarter cup of cognac. After the flame dies, remove the livers to a mixing bowl or food processor. Add an egg and three tablespoons of heavy cream. Mash thoroughly or process to make a pâté. Spoon some pâté onto each quail. Back in the frying pan, blend two tablespoons of flour into the drippings. Add a cup and a half of heavy cream and a quarter cup of cognac. Simmer, scraping the pan. Pour sauce into a blender, add an egg and some salt and pepper; whir away. Pour over pâté-topped quail. Bake at 350° for fifteen minutes. Serves six.

Quail with Goose Liver Pâté in a Cognac Cream Sauce

TURKEY

A couple of years ago, on May 22, I was doing my usual morning spot on the "Good Day! Live" show in Boston. It just happened that a group of people on the West Coast (where else?) had predicted the end of the world on that very day. About the same time, there were some problems with a nuclear reactor. Of course, a group of East Coast (where else?) people were predicting that it was going to "melt down" and start a chain reaction that would, naturally, bring about the end of the world. My first thought was, What do you cook for the end of the world? In honor of what could have become a very auspicious occasion, I opened the show with Turkey Meltdown.

Turkey Meltdown

Bone a turkey breast; simmer the bones (and skin) with a cup of water to make a simple stock for the sauce. Cube the turkey meat and shake the cubes in bread crumbs. Fry in about six tablespoons of butter, seasoning with salt, pepper, parsley, and thyme. When cubes are browned on all sides, splash with white wine. Simmer another five minutes and remove turkey from the pan. Pour the pan drippings into a blender. Arrange some tomato and zucchini wedges in the bottom of a bake-and-serve dish around a lone tomato slice. Build up a pile of turkey cubes and grated cheese on the vegetables. Top with whole mushrooms. Back in the blender, add two egg yolks and half a cup of turkey stock to the pan drippings. Pour the blended sauce over the mixture in the baking dish. Beat two egg whites until soft peaks form; sprinkle with salt and pepper. Pile this meringue around and on top of the turkey and vegetables. Decorate with more whole mushrooms. Bake at 325° for ten minutes. Reduce heat to 300° to bake thirty minutes more. This creation will swell to a puffy cloud, then "melt down" when served.

It is convenient to be able to now buy just the turkey breast. I actually prefer dark meat, but in the restaurant there are just some dishes best made using the breast. This is one.

**Turkey Breast
in a Champagne
Cream Sauce
with Crabmeat**

Smear a turkey breast with soft butter and sprinkle with salt, pepper, garlic, paprika, and parsley. Bake uncovered in a hot (500°) oven until it is browned. This should take about thirty minutes, but it really depends on the size; check the breast every fifteen minutes or so. Next, bathe the turkey with two cups of dry champagne and cover or seal with foil. Bake at 450° for another forty-five to ninety minutes, allowing about twenty minutes per pound. When done, remove the breast from the pan and scrape all the juices into a blender. Add two cups of heavy cream, one egg, and about a quarter cup of flour. Blend well, pour the sauce into a pan, and simmer for twenty to thirty minutes. If necessary, blend again to smooth. Fold in one pint of fresh crabmeat. Set the sauce aside. By this time the turkey should be cool enough to handle. Using your fingers, remove the bone (a simple procedure; just follow your instincts). Slice the breast meat into a bake-and-serve dish. Ladle with sauce, sprinkle with a cup or two of a grated mild cheese Muenster, Havarti, or a mild Cheddar), and bake at 400° for about ten minutes. Serve.

(Turkey Breast in a Champagne Cream Sauce with Crabmeat)

Meat

An almost complete lack of red meat is something new in my diet. This didn't happen suddenly; nothing mystical or even "humane" has prompted this change in my eating habits. My own body's declining need to digest red meat is the primary cause. We all know that our metabolism changes with age, making it unnecessary to eat certain foods.

Years ago when people labored hard and long at farming and heavy factory work, it would seem that we required the amount of substantial protein-filled food such as red meat that is habit still for many of us. And because the work was so much harder then, I think people were able to work all that through their systems. Today, it seems a simple case of overload.

I find it a real "socio-culinary" barometer watching the price of red meat (beef and lamb for instance) dropping while some fish (swordfish and salmon) have climbed to over six dollars a pound. People may be eating more fish and poultry because they simply cannot work off heavier meats.

In the restaurant business, however, it's difficult to just stop serving red meat. More important, nothing is a panacea. What works for me really only works for me. Anyway, I'm delighted to share what I know with those who can still eat meat and get away with it.

BEEF

You'll need to buy a tenderloin of beef; a whole one will cost in the neighborhood of thirty dollars. You should be able to get eight to ten cuts from it yourself, or ask your butcher for inch-thick beef fillets. If you do buy the whole tenderloin, be certain to peel the layer of fat from across the top and then slice it into your one-inch servings. Next you'll need filo dough and some goose liver pâté (page 14). Cover the top of each cut with pâté (about an inch thick is the way I like it). Then wrap in filo dough just like you'd wrap a sandwich in waxed paper. Slather the dough on all sides with softened butter and set on an oiled cookie sheet. Preheat oven to 500°, then bake the little Wellingtons for twelve to fifteen minutes. Transfer to a platter; add sauce and serve.

Mushroom Cognac Sauce Flambé: Melt one stick of butter in a frying pan. When it sizzles, add two cups sliced mushrooms, a half cup sliced shallots, a handful of fresh chopped parsley, four minced garlic cloves, and salt and black pepper to taste. Simmer until shallots are tender, then splash with a half cup of good cognac and tilt the pan to ignite. Now, do not dump your meal into the burner; a quick, slight tilt will do it. For the less deft, the faint at heart, or those not "cooking with gas," use a match! Pour flaming sauce across the Wellingtons. In any case, this is not a

Baby Beef Wellingtons

good sauce to make while wearing chiffon with puffy sleeves.

Sweet and Sour Tenderloin Pâté in Filo

Tenderloin pâté is simply a meat loaf made with expensive meat. You'll need a food processor for this feat. We'll fancy it up further by wrapping it in a flaky pastry. Start by cubing two pounds of beef tenderloin (even a lesser grade will work). Process the cubes with a stick of butter, two eggs, a half cup of chopped celery, four tablespoons beef bouillon, a quarter cup brandy, black pepper to taste, and a couple of hits of A-1 or Worcestershire sauce. Process just long enough to become smooth, but not much further as it has a tendency then to take on a chalky taste. Remove and lay on a counter. After working it into a long loaf shape, make a lengthwise indentation with the side of your hand. Press in whole cooked carrots and fresh raw mushrooms. Squeeze the top back together over the vegetables and wrap the loaf in a double sheet of buttered filo dough. Cut strips from another double sheet to braid and lay down the center of the loaf, using a touch of water to help the braid adhere. Bake on a cookie sheet in a preheated 400° oven for about half an hour. Slice and serve with sauce.

Sweet and Sour Tomato Sauce: Quickly saute a cup of chopped fresh tomatoes with a half cup of chopped onions, a quarter cup of sugar, a half cup of vinegar, and garlic and pepper to taste. (Have you noticed I don't make much without garlic and pepper?) Cook only until tomatoes and onions soften.

Beef Tenderloin in Filo with Shrimp and Artichoke Stuffing

Prepare tenderloin in the same fashion as the Wellingtons, slicing it into the same inch-thick pieces and spreading them with this shrimp and artichoke stuffing instead of pâté. Wrap in filo and bake in a preheated oven for twelve to fifteen minutes. Serve with hot Lemon Butter Cognac Sauce.

Stuffing: Shell, devein, and chop two pounds of raw shrimp. Set it into a bowl and add two drained cans (or fourteen to eighteen fresh) of artichoke hearts that have been cut lengthwise into halves. Mix in the juice of two lemons, six minced garlic cloves, one egg, salt and pepper to taste, and one-fourth cup each of chopped fresh parsley and melted butter. The stuffing is ready to pile onto your beef medallions.

Lemon Butter Cognac Sauce: In a saucepan melt one stick of butter. Add the juice of one lemon, a half cup of cognac, a quarter cup of chopped scallions, a tablespoon chopped garlic, and some salt and black pepper. Cook only long enough for scallions to soften, maybe fifteen minutes.

(Beef Tenderloin in Filo with Shrimp and Artichoke Stuffing)

Peel the fat from a whole tenderloin; rub with garlic and season with black pepper, paprika, and savory. Lay several bay leaves on top. Bake in a hot oven (500°) about ten minutes per pound. Remove and let stand ten to fifteen minutes. Then, with your knife held slightly at an angle, slice into inch-thick pieces and set aside. Letting the beef sit and cool somewhat before cutting keeps the juices from running; the meat seems more tender as a result. Don't even poke it with a fork.

Sauce: Slice a pound of bacon crossways before you cook it. This will not only give you instant bacon bits later, but it will cook more easily and more evenly. I always season bacon when I cook it because it is, after all, meat at two dollars a pound. Drain after cooking and set the meat aside. Discard the pan grease,

Beef Tenderloin Flambé in Bacon and Mushroom Brandy Sauce

(Beef Tenderloin Flambé in Bacon and Mushroom Brandy Sauce)

but don't wash the pan—you want to retain the bacon flavor. Melt a stick of butter in this pan, then slice in six shallots and two pounds of mushrooms. Add one-fourth cup chopped fresh parsley, some garlic and basil, and salt and pepper to taste. Simmer about ten minutes. Add the reserved bacon. Stir well and then make a hole in the center of the mixture by pushing aside the mushrooms and bacon. Lay your beef cuts in this ring and sear quickly on both sides. Splash with a half cup of brandy and ignite by tilting toward the flame or using a match (do read my precautionary note in the last recipe). Serve flaming.

I first got the idea of using peanut butter on food (other than Wonder bread with grape jelly) from an Indonesian chef named Su Yoo (sounds like an Oriental lawyer). He often served it as a sauce on skewered beef. In Indonesia people use peanut butter sauces on a lot of things, including their salad greens. Mine is an elegant wine-based sauce.

Beef Tenderloin in a Peanut Butter Sauce

Peel and discard the fat from a whole beef tenderloin. Season with pepper, garlic, and bay leaves and bake in a 500° oven for about ten minutes per pound. While it's cooking, prepare the following sauce.

Sauce: In a saucepan mix a stick of butter, two cups dry white wine, one cup creamy or crunchy peanut butter, and one tablespoon each of minced garlic and black pepper. Heat, stirring often. Add salt if needed. When beef is ready, slice and ladle with sauce to serve.

I know that my beef recipes are all for tenderloin, but that's what I like best. In fact, I don't cook anything else at the restaurant. On occasion I used to do a tenderloin strip or a prime rib, but as I explained earlier, my affinity for beef has waned. On the other hand, if I were simply cooking for myself or my family at home, I would certainly use other, more economical cuts of meat.

But whether it be tenderloin or a cheaper cut, buy a whole roast or ham or chicken—even if you live alone. Don't get caught in the movement toward single-serving portions or the school of thought that baking a small "snacking" cake is better than bothering with a "whole" cake. The cost to the consumer of all these individualized servings is frightening. With proper storage, albeit freezing, you can have a whole week's worth of food for almost nothing. A bottom or top round roast cooked with potatoes, carrots, onions, and gravy is terrific on Sunday. It's still more wonderful reheated on Tuesday, and practically an old friend when turned into a stew on Thursday. With any luck and ingenuity, it can be quite a soup on Saturday, too. As I often say, food costs have nothing to do with prices, and everything to do with imagination.

The media have promoted "individuality" for so long—frozen TV dinners, instant portions of one thing or another; they even hype pandering to individual tastes at the same meal—that the old concept of "leftovers" seems to have disappeared. Who today talks about cold mutton sandwiches, red flannel hash (page 86), or leftover ham with beans?

Here are some suggestions for large cuts of meat. They will not only save you money in the long run, but stretch your imagination as well. Following this selection of veal, pork, and lamb "roasts" are two ideas for the "leftovers."

ROASTS

Roast Leg of Veal in a Champagne and Bacon Cream Sauce

Starting with an eight-pound leg of veal (or anything in that neighborhood), salt and pepper it and sprinkle with fresh parsley. Roast, uncovered in a baking pan, at 500° for forty-five minutes. Drain off grease, douse with a quart of white wine, and cover the top with onion slices. Cover tightly with foil and return to oven, lowering temperature to 450°. Bake for another

(Roast Leg of Veal in a Champagne and Bacon Cream Sauce)

sixty to ninety minutes. Veal should not be rare; it should be more on the well-done side.

Sauce: While veal is roasting, slice a pound of bacon crossways into little squares and fry. Set bacon bits aside; drain off grease but do not wash pan. Melt a stick of butter in this pan, then slowly smooth in a quarter cup of flour for thickening. Stir in two cups of champagne and two cups of "half and half." Season with salt, pepper, summer savory, and parsley. Simmer, stirring well, until the sauce thickens like a gravy. If it's not thick enough, add a touch more flour; if too thick, add more cream or champagne. Finally, add the bacon and simmer the sauce for another fifteen minutes. Slice the roasted veal, lay it in a bake-and-serve dish, cover with sauce, and bake at 400° for half an hour. Serve.

For variety, do everything the same except add two cups of fresh crabmeat to the bacon champagne cream sauce or add artichoke hearts or two cups chopped watercress or one cup slivered almonds or two cups sliced fresh peaches or apples or any combination of fresh fruits. You might add a cup of any pesto (pages 82–84). The possibilities are endless—and that's true with everything.

Veal Roast in a Curried Tomato–Sour Cream Sauce

Rub a leg or rump roast with salt, pepper, and garlic. Bake in a preheated 500° oven for thirty minutes. Drain off grease, baste generously with a couple of cups of white wine, cover, and return to a 450° oven. Roast, allowing twenty minutes per pound.

Sauce: Melt half a stick of butter in a saucepan. Blend in four tablespoons of flour and two tablespoons of curry powder. Then add four chopped, ripe red tomatoes and two cups of sour cream. Transfer to a blender to smooth. Slice the roast veal into a bake-and-serve dish. Stir any of the roasting pan juices into the sour cream sauce, then pour over the meat slices. Garnish with tomato slices. Return to a 400° oven and bake another fifteen to twenty minutes.

Roast Pork with Fruit and Sausage in Orange Brandy Sauce

Have your butcher bone and "butterfly" a pork loin. It should lie flat and be about an inch thick. The ones I use seem to measure fourteen to eighteen inches long and ten to twelve inches wide. Cover the meat with any mixture of dried pitted fruit that you prefer. (Caution: cooked papaya takes on a strange odor.) I have successfully used combinations that included apricots, mangoes, dates, currants, and dried pineapple. Any large and ungainly pieces can be pruned. You could also choose to go with a single dried fruit, say prunes. After you've laid out the fruit, spread sausage meat on top. Again, the choice is entirely up to you. With the particular fruits mentioned above, I have used Portuguese linguica, sweet Italian or Polish sausage, or a combination. Tightly roll the loin lengthwise and tie it at two-inch intervals. Salt and pepper the loin and stuff a bay leaf under the string at each tied spot. Bake uncovered in a preheated 500° oven for thirty minutes to seal in the juices. Drain grease, splash with two cups of white wine, cover tightly, and return to a 450° oven for one hour and fifteen minutes. Remove and let sit twenty minutes before slicing. Set slices in a bake-and-serve dish, pour orange brandy sauce over the stuffed meat, and bake another ten to fifteen minutes.

Orange Brandy Sauce: Blend a half cup of orange marmalade with one cup each of brandy, Dijon mustard, and frozen orange concentrate. Add a teaspoon of dill, and some black pepper and garlic to taste. Simmer this sauce for thirty minutes before baking with stuffed loin slices as directed above.

When preparing stuffed rolled meat, you'll find it easier to deal with if you cook it a day in advance and then slice it cold. It can also be served cold.

The basic directions for stuffed loins always remain the same, only the stuffing changes—not unlike life. Stuffing meats offers a wonderful, and for some, a new approach to the same old thing. Here are three more ideas that are definitely not the same old thing.

Roast Pork Stuffed with Fiddlehead Fern Pesto

Cover the boned and butterflied loin with a thick layer of fiddlehead fern pesto (page 83), roll tightly, and tie. Bake as directed in the preceding recipe, ladling the stuffed slices with this cognac mushroom sauce before returning to the oven for the final cooking.

Cognac Mushroom Sauce: After the initial baking stage, drain the white wine juices from the pan into a blender. Add a cup of cognac, a tablespoon of flour, and salt and black pepper to taste. Blend smooth, pour into a saucepan, and stir in half a pound of sliced mushrooms. Simmer about twenty minutes or until mushrooms are done to your liking. Add chopped fresh parsley.

Roast Pork Stuffed with Apples and Parsnips

Spread the boned and butterflied loin with this parsnip and apple filling: mix two cups each of chopped, unpeeled, scrubbed parsnips and cored apples with one cup of chopped onion, two eggs, a quarter cup of minced parsley, three tablespoons each of marjoram and thyme, and salt and black pepper to taste. Roll, tie, bake, douse with wine, rebake, let sit, and slice— all as directed in the first recipe for roast pork. Prepare this cranberry sauce while the meat is cooking; then pour over the slices before the final ten to fifteen minutes in the oven.

Cranberry Grand Marnier Sauce: Simmer in a

saucepan one cup of frozen orange concentrate, one cup maple syrup, a quarter cup of prepared mustard, and two cups of fresh cranberries. When the cranberries begin to pop and soften, stir in one cup of Grand Marnier.

(Roast Pork
Stuffed with Apples
and Parsnips)

Try this some blustery winter evening! As in the preceding recipes, start with a boned and butterflied pork loin and spread it with this hearty stuffing: thin-slice two cups each of potatoes and cabbage. Add one cup of chopped onion, and salt, black pepper, and garlic to taste. Roll, tie, and bake as directed previously, but splash with four cups of burgundy (blended with two tablespoons of flour) instead of white wine. Throw in a pound of sliced mushrooms and a half cup of sauerkraut. Cover and continue with the second baking stage; the sauce forms in the bottom of the pan.

**Roast Pork with
Cabbage, Potatoes,
and Burgundy
Sauerkraut**

Rub down a six-pound leg of lamb with a mixture of olive oil, garlic, and soy sauce. Then pepper it and bake it in a preheated 500° oven for about thirty minutes. This seals in the juices. Drain grease and baste with two cups of dry white wine. Cover and bake another forty-five to sixty minutes. While leg cools enough to handle, prepare curried tomatoes. Then slice meat from bone, cover meat with sauce, and serve.

**Leg of Lamb
with Curried
Green Tomatoes**

Curried Green Tomatoes with Maple Syrup: Melt about a tablespoon of bacon fat in a skillet. When it's sizzling, chop in two large green tomatoes and one medium onion. Stir in a half cup of maple syrup, the juice of one lemon, and two tablespoons of vinegar. Sprinkle with one tablespoon of hot curry powder (Madras is a hot one) and salt, pepper, and garlic to taste. Simmer twenty minutes.

WHAT TO DO WITH LEFTOVERS

Any leftover meat (from the preceding seven recipes, for example) can be ground and seasoned, an egg or two added, rolled into a ball or shaped into a patty, and either fried or baked. You choose the accompanying sauce. I call them fricadelles; it's a name I discovered in an old cookbook. Stir-frying is another satisfying solution.

Veal Fricadelles with Raisins

Mix four cups of ground leftover veal with one cup of raisins, one tablespoon of chopped garlic, a handful of chopped fresh parsley, and salt and pepper to taste. Roll into little meatballs, fry in butter, and serve with Kirsch and Brandy Barbecue Sauce (page 87).

Lamb Stir-Fry with Scallions and Pears

Slice fresh or leftover lamb as thinly as you can, removing as much fat as possible. Chop and set aside one-half cup of a mixture of fresh basil, marjoram, and mint. (I grow an herb called "orange mint" and it really is. If you have orange mint, this would be an ideal place to enjoy it.) Prepare and set aside a half cup of chopped scallions and two thin-sliced wonderful pears. (I say "wonderful," but unless you're picking them off your own tree, the chances are mighty slim. Everything is shipped green these days, so they're usually hard when you buy them and by the time they have ripened sitting in a paper bag in a dark closet, what you have is fruit-flavored disappointment.) Heat four tablespoons of sesame oil in a large skillet or wok. Fling in your strips of lamb first, salt and pepper them, and add four chopped cloves of garlic and the herb mixture. Turn the lamb, just browning it on both sides; then add two tablespoons crème de cassis. Add scallions and pear slices, stir-fry, splash with soy sauce, and sprinkle with half a cup of grated coconut (optional). Serve.

STUFFED VEAL

Getting back to wonderful pears, towns ought to plant fruit trees up and down the streets and let the people reap the harvest. Free fresh fruit—a place could seem like Eden. And where would we be without apples?

Veal Cutlets Stuffed with Apple in a Walnut-Cheese Sauce

Slice eight very thin cutlets, salt and pepper both sides, and set aside. (You will serve two of these stuffed slivers per person, so this recipe serves four.) Stuff with a mixture of three chopped (cored but not peeled) apples, two eggs, salt, pepper, and thyme. Wrap each cutlet around a portion of the stuffing and fasten with a toothpick. Bake uncovered at 500° for thirty minutes. Drain any juices into the sauce, stir well, pour sauce over stuffed veal, and sprinkle with parsley and minced walnuts. Bake another fifteen to twenty minutes at 400°. Serve.

Sauce: Simmer in a saucepan two cups of Gourmandaise walnut cheese, one cup each of dry white wine and light cream, an egg, a quarter cup of flour, a shake of white pepper, one tablespoon each of basil and chives, and the juices from the cooked stuffed cutlets. Once the cheese is melted, smooth the sauce in a blender, then pour over the cutlets. Continue baking as directed.

Veal Cutlets Stuffed with Artichoke and Pimiento

Slice fifteen to eighteen artichoke hearts (canned or fresh) into halves lengthwise. Toss with two chopped pimientos, two eggs, a half cup melted butter, and one tablespoon each of tarragon and chopped fresh chives. Season with salt, pepper, and garlic. Using toothpicks to hold them together, roll the cutlets around this stuffing and lay them in a bake-and-serve dish. Bake uncovered in a 500° oven for twenty

(Veal Cutlets Stuffed with Artichoke and Pimiento)

minutes, then drain juices into the sauce. Pour sauce back over the cutlets and bake in a somewhat cooler oven (400°) for another twenty to thirty minutes.

White Vermouth Cream Sauce: Whip in a blender two cups of light cream and a half cup of white vermouth with an egg, a quarter cup of flour, a pimiento, four tablespoons of snipped fresh parsley, a teaspoon of chopped garlic, salt and white pepper to taste, and the pan juices from the baked cutlets.

Vegetables

Everyone knows that you should "eat your vegetables." They provide vitamins, minerals, and the all-important bulk (now called fiber by food freaks like me) in our diet. Too many people are stuffing themselves instead with "lite" food—and getting "lite" results. Someone once suggested that I go on a low-carbohydrate diet, which means lots of flesh and little fruit or vegetables. They said that I would lose weight fast. I didn't. I felt constantly deprived, and I was cranky and melancholy to boot. Naturally I quit it!

In the book of Genesis (1:29-30), God Himself tells us that He has given us herbs and the fruit of the earth as our meat. There's some difference of opinion about the translation of the word "meat," but whatever the interpretation, who can refuse such colorful gifts? And speaking of colorful, you could almost use the first recipe of this chapter as a centerpiece; it's sure to delight even hardcore vegetable haters.

Cauliflower Crown

Wash a whole cauliflower and remove the leaves. Cut the bottom flat so that it stands on its own; then butter, salt, and pepper it. Using toothpicks as skewers, decorate your "crown" with cherry tomatoes, celery chunks, zucchini cubes, broccoli flowerettes, eggplant squares, onion rings, and so on. Stick these "jewels," with or without a pattern, all over the cauliflower. Drizzle melted butter (seasoned with salt, pepper, and garlic) all over the head. Cover gently with foil and bake at 400° for about forty minutes.

When we serve a variety of vegetables at the restaurant, we generally bake them as an oven "ratatouille." Yet baking takes time, and at home you could prepare that same bunch of vegetables on top of the stove—braised in a dutch oven, stir-fried, deep-fried, just plain fried, or steamed. And, now that so many people have a machine that does all the cutting and shredding, the entire process can be scaled down to a few moments. This mixed vegetable idea is really my favorite food. Besides, a fantastic-tasting combination such as carrots, broccoli, zucchini, tomatoes and eggplant—with or without cheese—becomes a wonderfully complete dinner filled with nearly all the nutrients that preserve and promote a happy and healthy life—not bad for the humble fruit of the earth. Here are a few stir-fry suggestions that do not need a wok, only a large hot pan.

STIR-FRIED VEGETABLES

Zucchini and Spinach with Nasturtiums

Shred four zucchini, toss them into four tablespoons of sizzling olive oil. Add one pound of washed uncut spinach, salt and pepper to taste, and two good handfuls of nasturtium blossoms. Stir-fry until spinach wilts.

Dandelion Greens and Cucumbers

Peel and thin-slice two large cucumbers. Plop them with a good bunch of young dandelion leaves and a couple of cloves of garlic into some hot olive oil. Sprinkle with salt, pepper, and basil. It's practically done already!

Chop a half cup each of eggplant, tomatoes, celery, and mushrooms. Toss into a couple of tablespoons of hot olive oil. Season generously with salt, pepper, garlic, and basil; add one-half cup of tomato paste. Stir-fry for about six minutes. It's a wonderful combination to serve cold as an antipasto, or hot over pasta. It makes a good side dish, or even a main dish.

(Dandelion Greens and Cucumbers)

Eggplant and Tomatoes

BEET GREENS AND OTHER LEAVES

Wash them, chop them (or don't bother), and sauté them—deep dark greens seem best in bacon fat, ham grease, or olive oil. A little salt and pepper could be added, but I almost never add herbs or spices to any green vegetable because I think they are an herb by themselves.

This applies to all green leafy vegetables (cabbage, kale, spinach, collards, and so on)—maybe add a little chopped onion here and there, but that's enough. Don't cook them too long either—only until they have wilted and are hot. Taste, as well as nutrition, is the reason.

CARROTS

There are not many ways to cut a carrot. You can slice, dice, quarter, julienne it. You can leave it whole. They are all wonderful. With this fact established, I'll give you the basics of carrot cookery. First, do not peel them; a quick scrubbing will do. Cut (see above), lay in a baking dish, cover with a sauce (aha! the trick), cover or seal tightly with foil, and bake at 400° for about forty-five minutes.

**Carrots in
Curry Catsup**

Blend a half cup of melted butter with one cup of cat-sup, a tablespoon of curry powder, and a half cup of dry white wine. Pour over carrots and bake.

Carrots in Root Beer

So simple—pour a bottle of root beer over your car-rots, dot with butter, and sprinkle brown sugar across the top. Bake.

The "Carrots in Root Beer" concept lends itself well to ginger ale, cream soda (especially nice on parsnips), sarsaparilla, and Moxie. Dr. Pepper junkies, like my brother, can even use that, although I'm not certain that I approve.

**Carrots in Frangelico
and Coffee**

Mix two cups of strong coffee with one cup of Fran-gelico, a half cup of melted butter, a dash of cinna-mon, and a half cup of honey. Bake.

**Sweet and Sour
Carrots with
Bacon and Onions**

Dice, then fry a half pound of bacon, throwing in a cup of diced onions to cook along with the meat. Set bacon and onion bits aside and add four tablespoons of bacon fat to a blender. Blend with a half cup each of vinegar and maple syrup. Season to taste with salt, black pepper, and caraway. Bake, then serve topped with bacon and onion bits.

CELERY

Walking in New York City years ago, I couldn't resist a hotel sign that advertised "Spiritualists' Convention, Second Floor Ball-room." Upstairs, a seer was telling a woman who suffered from arthritis, "The spirit tells me that you should eat celery, a lot of celery—tea from celery seeds, stuffed celery, celery soup, celery everything, go on a celery binge." I don't know if celery would really help arthritis, but it tastes good. Of course, it is true that certain plants contain substances common to some pain-killing remedies.

Celery Patties

Grate (or shred in a processor) one bunch of celery. Drain off the juice and reserve for the sauce below. Add two eggs and a half cup of flour or bread crumbs to the celery. Mix in a quarter cup of chopped onion, two tablespoons of melted butter, one tablespoon of chicken bouillon, a teaspoon of thyme, and a half teaspoon of nutmeg. Once thoroughly combined, form into patties and dust with bread crumbs. Fry in butter, browning on both sides. Remove to a bake-and-serve dish and prepare sauce.

Sour Cream Sauce: Blend the reserved celery juice and two tablespoons of flour into a half cup of sour cream. Season with salt and pepper. Pour over patties and bake in a 400° oven for about twenty minutes.

Celery Pudding

Whip in a blender until smooth: two cups chopped celery, one cup honey, one-half cup frozen orange concentrate, four egg yolks, and two envelopes of gelatin. Pour into a saucepan and simmer until thick. Blend again to smooth any lumps. Let cool. Whip the four egg whites, fold them into the cooled pudding, and pour into serving dishes to cool completely and set.

Stuffed Celery Knobs

The knob is the last three or four inches of the celery head. Wash the knobs, then steam them in white wine for twenty minutes. You will now be able to spread the softened sections and press in the Bread Stuffing. Bake at 400° for fifteen minutes.

Bread Stuffing: Mix together bread crumbs, softened butter, a dash of olive oil, Parmesan cheese, lemon juice, and oregano.

TOMATOES

Tomatoes have been fondly considered "love apples" by the Italians and French and regarded accordingly by others as sinful. As a kid I would only eat them sprinkled with sugar. It's funny how different people regard tomatoes. There's even a chef in Maine whose fame is built upon a dislike of tomatoes.

Sweet and Sour Fried Green Tomatoes

Slice green tomatoes about half an inch thick, dip in beaten egg and then in flour, and fry in butter until browned on both sides. Salt and pepper both sides as they are cooking. Then sprinkle with one-half cup brown sugar, a couple of tablespoons of chopped onion, and one-quarter cup white vinegar. Dust with garlic powder and dill. Serve.

Baked Tomatoes in Orange Marmalade and Cointreau

Serve this one hot or cold. Slice tomatoes into a bake-and-serve dish. Pour sauce over and season with some salt and pepper. Bake at 400° for thirty minutes, or don't bake and serve them cold.

Sauce: Mix one-half cup Cointreau into one cup of orange marmalade. Season with a tablespoon of tarragon.

Baked Tomatoes in Sambuca and Lemon Herb Butter

Cut tops from tomatoes, line them up in a baking dish, pour over the sauce, and bake at 400° for thirty minutes.

Sauce: Blend one-quarter cup of Sambuca with four tablespoons each of melted butter and honey, one tablespoon of mixed fresh herbs, and the juice of one lemon.

This same sauce can be adapted for a variety of tastes, depending on your imagination and courage. Instead of Sambuca you might try crème de cassis, apricot brandy, coffee brandy, or raspberry or cranberry liqueurs. (Check out the two baked tomato recipes in the "Fast Food" chapter.) The combinations are almost unlimited.

POTATOES

Sweet Potatoes Stuffed with Bacon and Collards

(Diced tofu and olive oil can be substituted for the bacon.) Bake three large sweet potatoes at 400° until soft, about forty-five minutes. Then cut them in half lengthwise so that the potato half can sit by itself. Scoop out the inside and save. Dice, then fry a pound of bacon until crisp. Set the bacon bits aside and drain all but four tablespoons of grease. In that fat, sauté four cups of chopped collard greens for about six minutes. Stir in the reserved potato and bacon; stuff the mixture back into the potato skins. Top with buttered bread crumbs and dried currants. Bake or broil just long enough to brown the top.

Curried Sweet Potato and Cranberry Swirl

Bake six large sweet potatoes at 400° until they are soft in the center, about forty-five minutes. Scoop potato out of the skins into a mixing bowl. Whip smooth with one egg, one-half cup brown sugar, one-quarter cup frozen orange concentrate, and two tablespoons curry. In a saucepan, stir one pound of cranberries into a cup each of maple syrup, Amaretto, and walnuts. Boil until cranberries soften, adding more maple syrup if it's not yet sweet enough for your taste. Swirl the cooked mixture into the mashed sweet potatoes. Bake ten minutes at 400°, then serve.

The following New England Sweet Potato Crown seems complicated at first glance, but it has always been a success for me. Just gather what you'll need beforehand: a six-to-eight inch soufflé dish, two jars of spiced apple rings and a jar of whole spiced apples, a half pound of softened butter, and some cooled cooked cranberries, parsnips, and sweet potatoes. I'll tell you how to prepare the last three items in the recipe.

New England Sweet Potato Crown

Preparation: Cook one cup of cranberries in maple syrup (or brown sugar and water) just long enough to soften and sweeten. Simmer four peeled and julienned parsnips in butter, salt, and pepper until soft, about twenty minutes. Bake about ten to twelve sweet potatoes until soft, spoon out of the skins, and mash with a touch of nutmeg (you should end up with four to six cups mashed).

Setting up the "crown": Thickly butter the inside of the soufflé dish. This will act as a "paste" for the vegetables. Lay a ring of cranberries around the base of the dish right where the floor and wall meet. Inside the ring of cranberries, overlap apple rings to form a circle. Cut some apple rings to match your julienned parsnips and stick them both around the side of the dish in some pattern of your own design. Do make the arrangement as tight as you can. Carefully plaster the bottom and sides with the mashed sweet potatoes. Fill the center with two or three spiced whole apples. Cover the apples with more sweet potato, packing it down to fill the dish. Bake in a preheated 425° oven for twenty minutes. Turn it upside down on a cake plate and gently lift the dish off the crown. This never fails (for me).

Roast Potatoes in a Bacon Cream Sauce

To serve six, use three large potatoes, one pound of bacon, and one pint of light cream. Dice and fry bacon in a drizzle of oil, seasoning it with salt, pepper, garlic, parsley, and basil. Remove bacon from pan and set aside. Drain all but four tablespoons of grease from the skillet; stir in two tablespoons of flour to make a paste. Add the light cream, one-half cup of dry sherry, a half cup of chopped scallions, two tablespoons chopped parsley, and salt and pepper to taste. Simmer sauce until creamy and thick. Add the reserved bacon, stir well, and pour over sliced potatoes (leave the skins off if you like) in a baking dish. Bake uncovered at 400° for forty-five to sixty minutes.

(Roast Potatoes in a Bacon Cream Sauce)

Peel and boil enough potatoes for the number of people you want to serve. Mash and whip the cooked potatoes, adding some butter, salt, pepper, and parsley. Spoon into a soufflé or other baking dish and smooth the top. Cover with one-quarter to one-half inch of grated Havarti cheese and then cover that with a layer of pesto (see pages 82-84). Bake at 500° for twenty minutes. Chill, slice it as a pie, and serve for lunch or snack.

Potatoes with Cheese and Pesto

WILD RICE

I buy my wild rice from a company in Minnesota that is owned and managed by Indians. Wild rice is indigenous to North America, and since the Indians gave it to us, I feel that buying from them is good business.

Directions for wild rice often call for four or five cups of water for each cup of rice. I like three cups of white wine and half a cup of herb butter, one chopped onion, a taste of chicken bouillon, and perhaps some other fresh herbs. Drop the rice into boiling flavored liquid, cover, and reduce heat. Simmer, stirring occasionally, for forty-five to sixty minutes. Try stirring in vegetables, tofu, fried chicken livers, or whatever for the last fifteen minutes. Or, add cooked rice to the cream soup recipe (page 22).

Wild rice is the sort of thing that you can make a lot of and refrigerate. Later, mix it with whatever you want. Cold wild rice mixed with a fresh pesto makes a great salad for a one-dish lunch. Heat it up, add it to a pesto or stir-fried combination, and you've got dinner for four people in ten minutes. Nothing should take longer to cook than it does to eat.

These recipes are all for vegetables alone. But fruit cooked alongside vegetables not only makes the dish more interesting but healthful as well. Apples sliced with sweet potatoes, turnips, carrots, or lima beans has worked well for me. Raisins and coconut mixed in with peas, broccoli, spinach, or greens is a real treat as is a fiddle-head ferns and cantaloupe duo, rhubarb cooked with parsnips or asparagus, or dandelion leaves fried with pear slices in butter. It doesn't end. Eat your vegetables—and fruits.

Fast Food

For the past few years I've had the good fortune to be a regular chef on Boston's "Good Day! Live," a morning television talk show from station WCVB. For years in New York City I had struggled as a writer and actor trying to get into show business. People kept telling me I needed "an act." Then one day I gave it all up and started cooking. I realized that I finally had an act—and the restaurant was my stage. The next thing I knew, I was cooking on television. You always get what you order, eventually, even though you might not recognize the wrappings.

As a television chef, I've had to get up at four A.M., pull myself and the food together, and drive seventy miles in early commuter traffic; then fix a dish that was tantalizing, unique, nutritious, inexpensive, and so appealing that a hundred thousand people would write in for the recipe that day—and all in eight minutes! Everybody has crazy days just like that into which they're somehow supposed to fit whipping up a wonderful meal in minutes. That's why my television act is constantly a challenge. If I can do it in three steps instead of nine, so can you.

In developing these eight-minute demonstrations, I've reaffirmed my belief in using fresh, whole foods. There's nothing simpler, more logical, or more economical. If cooking were transportation, it would still be a horse-drawn carriage. That's how far behind we are. Most culinary schools are so in love with the ritual of technique that it is not surprising that so many people prefer convenience food (often at the expense of taste, health, creativity, and their wallet) to the long, arduous task of a complicated recipe. Even the "new cuisines" take an hour of preparation before the actual cooking begins. If we can fly from continent to continent in two hours, why can't we cook entire dinners, starting with fresh whole foods, in fifteen minutes or eight or even five? Well, we can, and I often do. I'm not talking about microwave meals. I don't own a microwave oven; I don't want one. I can do it faster in a hot pan.

Now, nothing gives me greater pleasure than to spend two days in the preparation of a holiday meal, and on the days I cook dinner at the restaurant, I often go in mid-morning just to have that extra time by myself to play with the food—"churning" a new flavored butter, trying out herbs from my garden, creating a sauce or a salad dressing. It relaxes me; it's my meditation, my therapy. Then there are the days when I simply want to throw it all in a pan and eat it —except that somewhere between the throwing and the eating, there ought to be a little brilliance.

This chapter contains thirty-six shining examples. They are all either ready-to-eat in eight minutes or can be prepared in eight minutes and forgotten about while they cook or chill. If I can do it on television, you should certainly be able to do it in the privacy of your own kitchen.

Ham, Sweet Potato, and Zucchini   Into a hot pan shred a small sweet potato; add a ham steak and some thin slices of zucchini. Salt and pepper what you'd like and brown the ham and vegetables.

Drizzle the sweet potatoes with maple syrup and baste the ham with a good shot of brandy. Serve.

(Ham, Sweet Potato, and Zucchini)

Heat butter in the bottom of a skillet until it sizzles. Add a boned and skinned chicken breast. Over that grate one zucchini and add about a cup of chopped or sliced mushrooms and half a square of tofu cut into bite-sized pieces. Sprinkle with some salt, pepper, garlic, and thyme. Cook about two minutes at medium-high heat. Then turn the chicken breast, stir the vegetables and tofu, and splash in about half a cup of white wine. Cook another three or four minutes. Serves two.

Chicken Breast with Tofu, Mushrooms, and Zucchini

Pasta, mixed with the right sauce, can be an almost instant no-work, convenient meal. It's good cold in a salad as well as hot. And the sauce ingredients can make a plate or bowl of pasta a healthful and complete meal. There seems to be more of a choice these days in pasta for those who love it, but hesitate to eat it for one reason or another. There are a lot of whole-grain pastas, high-protein pastas, and even a brand made from Jerusalem artichokes for people who are allergic to wheat.

Here is one elegant sauce for hot pasta; it's especially good tossed with tomato-flavored fettucine.

Grate two cups of Havarti cheese into a saucepan; stir in a cup of light cream, a quarter cup of cognac, two tablespoons of chopped garlic, a good tablespoon of black pepper, and some salt and fresh tarragon. Stirring almost constantly, let the sauce simmer until all the cheese has melted. Run it through a blender, adding one egg in the process. Pour it back into the saucepan and add one pound of fresh lobster meat cut into generous chunks. Simmer for a few minutes more, then toss with pasta and serve.

Lobster and Havarti Cognac Cream Sauce

Pesto is a favorite pasta sauce, a specialty of Genoa, Italy. Traditionally it is made with lots of fresh basil and garlic, worked in a mortar with grated Parmesan or pecorino sardo cheese and pounded pignoli nuts, blissfully bound together with olive oil.

It is healthy, luscious, elegant, and done the traditional way, would take you an hour to prepare. Not only that, if you couldn't get fresh basil (not to mention pecorino sardo or pignoli nuts), you'd be out of luck. Tradition, as I often say, hampers progress, and here we see that it limits what you can have for supper.

The solution is simple. Green is green, cheese is cheese, and nuts are nuts. Everyone has oil and garlic around the kitchen.

Spinach and Walnut Pesto

With your chopper blade in place, add to your food processor half a pound of trimmed spinach, half a cup of shelled walnuts, a cup of grated Havarti cheese, four to six cloves of garlic (or three tablespoons of garlic paste), half a cup of olive oil, two tablespoons of fresh chopped basil, one tablespoon of marjoram, and black pepper and salt to taste. Spin until all the ingredients are thoroughly blended, stopping just before the spinach becomes pureed, about forty-five seconds—no cooking involved!

While you were doing this you could have dropped a pound of fresh pasta into boiling water. It cooks in three minutes, so by the time you drain the noodles and toss them with your pesto sauce, you have a great dinner for four that probably took all of ten minutes. You could also prepare it all ahead of time and serve it chilled as a salad; remember to toss again before serving. Now that you've got the idea, here are a few more combinations.

Collard Green, Pecan, and Cheddar Pesto

Process about forty-five seconds, stopping just before the pesto becomes pureed: a cup of olive oil, half a pound of chopped raw collard greens, three-fourths of a cup of pecans, a cup of grated Cheddar, four to six garlic cloves, a tablespoon each of summer savory and sweet basil, and black pepper to taste.

Beet Green, Cashew, and Havarti Pesto

Grate a cup of Havarti cheese into the processor. Add eight to twelve tablespoons of olive oil, half a pound of chopped raw beet greens, half a cup of cashews, four to six cloves of garlic, one-fourth of a cup of grated Parmesan, two tablespoons chopped fresh basil, one tablespoon of thyme, and black pepper to taste. Process about forty-five seconds and toss immediately with hot pasta.

Watercress, Macadamia Nut, and Jarlsberg Pesto

Grate a cup of Jarlsberg cheese into a food processor; then spin for forty-five seconds with a cup of oil, four cups of chopped watercress, three-fourths of a cup of macadamia nuts, four to six cloves of garlic, one-fourth cup of grated Parmesan, two tablespoons of tarragon, one tablespoon of sweet basil, and black pepper to taste.

Fiddlehead Fern Pesto

Wash a couple of handfuls of fiddlehead ferns; defuzz and chop them into about four cups of smaller pieces. Cube about eight ounces of sharp yellow Cheddar and about the same quantity of a mild Muenster. Process the cheese with the fiddlehead fern pieces, a cup of olive oil, half a cup of black walnuts, the juice of one lemon, four to six garlic cloves, two tablespoons each of sage, basil, and parsley, and one tablespoon of black pepper. Process just until it begins to form a paste. Served on hot noodles with a glass of dandelion wine and a honey custard, it would make an incredible dinner, especially for Raggedy Ann and Andy.

A formula seems to emerge for what I call pesto. Process a cup each of oil and grated cheese with half a pound of chopped raw "green," flavoring it with four to six cloves of garlic, a few tablespoons of herbs, and a dusting of black pepper. Or, try spices and let me know how you like it.

Of course, there's the inevitable tomato sauce for pasta. Once at a department-store cooking demonstration, I was about to embark on my four-minute spaghetti sauce, when I spied the raised eyebrows of an Italian grandmother who assured me of her tomato sauce-making prowess and dared me to continue the demonstration. Much to her astonishment, and my relief, she admitted that, although it wasn't as traditional as her mother's, it nonetheless was delicious. Don't expect the same kind of taste that you get from simmering it for hours, but just taste this sauce for itself and maybe think of it as hot tomato pesto.

Fast Spaghetti Sauce

Cover the bottom of a frying pan with olive oil. Slice into the hot oil three ripe red tomatoes, a small green pepper, and a small onion. Stir-fry for one minute. Add three tablespoons each of garlic powder, basil, and Italian seasoning. Dust with black pepper. Then add half a cup of grated parmesan, and one to two cups of grated Havarti, Swiss, Muenster, or cheese of your choice. Stir-fry for another minute. Ladle across cooked pasta and serve.

Fish is a fast food favorite. The less you cook it, the better. In fact, you can eat it raw—see the sushi suggestions in the fish chapter. The first of the four fish recipes that I've gathered here has a special memory associated with it. I saw my first Broadway musical (*The Pajama Game*) as a seventeen-year-old runaway in New York City. Janis Paige sang her way into my heart that night. Visiting in Los Angeles twenty-five years later, my friend Kelly asked if I would cook dinner for Patti Page. No big deal, I thought, and then the expected guest turned out to be the fondly remembered Janis! This is what I served.

(Begin sauce first.) Slice three pounds of shark into pieces one-half inch thick; cut these into two-inch squares. Shake the cubes in flour and fry in hot butter until lightly browned on both sides. Sprinkle with salt, pepper, tarragon, and the juice of one lemon; splash with about a quarter cup of cognac (brandy will do). Arrange nicely with eight to ten artichoke hearts in a bake-and-serve dish. Pour the sauce over and bake in a 400° oven for about twelve minutes.

Sauce: Blend a cup of grated Havarti cheese with three-fourths of a cup each of sour and heavy cream, one-half cup each of dry sherry and white wine, one egg, four cloves of crushed garlic, two tablespoons each of chicken bouillon and flour, one teaspoon of tarragon, a sprinkling of white pepper and the pan juices from the fried fish. When creamy, pour into a saucepan and stir in four or five broken artichoke hearts. Simmer for six to eight minutes, stirring often. Pour over fish and bake as directed.

Shark Janis Paige

Into a hot skillet, the bottom covered with olive oil, add one-half pound each of chopped fresh cod, raw peeled shrimp, one chopped tomato, one chopped onion, half a cup of chopped crabmeat, one cup each of dry sherry and clam broth. Season with salt and pepper. Serve with a bottle of white wine, Emerald City Salad (page 33), and a loaf of sourdough bread.

Eight-Minute Fish Stew

Butter, flour, salt, and pepper six trout both inside and out. Wash and chop about a head of romaine lettuce; season it with salt, pepper, and tarragon, and sprinkle with lemon juice and white wine. Add one egg and a handful of breadcrumbs. Stuff the mixture into the fish cavities. Lay the stuffed fish in a baking

Trout Stuffed with Romaine

(Trout Stuffed with Romaine)

dish and pour over a sauce made up of a stick of melted butter, the juice of one lemon, four tablespoons of cognac, salt, pepper, and garlic. Bake at 400° for about twenty minutes. Serve.

Smoked Trout in a Cheese Custard

Lift the bone out of six smoked trout fillets and lay in a ten-to-twelve inch unbaked pie shell. Blend together six eggs, two cups of grated cheese (Swiss, Muenster, Havarti, or something else), and one-half cup each of dry sherry and light cream. Season with salt, white pepper, and tarragon. Pour this custard mixture over the trout. Bake ten minutes at 400°; reduce heat to 325° and cook forty minutes more. Serve hot or cold.

New England Red Flannel Hash is called red flannel hash because it looks like red flannel. I tell you, New Englanders are brilliant! If this dish had happened on the West Coast, they would have called it Natural Granola Borscht Loaf, and served it with carrot cake.

New England Red Flannel Hash

Combine one and a half cups each of leftover meat and chopped cooked beets with three cups of chopped cooked potatoes, one small diced onion, about a quarter cup of diced cooked bacon with drippings, two tablespoons of Worcestershire sauce, and salt and pepper to taste. Add enough light cream to bind it together. Spread it in a frying pan, and cook until the underside begins to brown, then fold it over like an omelet.

Or, shape the hash into a loaf on a baking sheet. Set sliced apple halves around it and sprinkle the apples with cinnamon, sugar, and nutmeg. Bake uncovered at 400° for forty minutes.

Apples make great stuffings and you can use them for more than you might expect. For a fast meal, roll an apple stuffing into a chicken breast or lay strips of turkey, veal, or fish into a crepe with it. Sauté or bake the breast or crepe in a sauce. You could even stuff a fish with it or fish fillets, or stuff a tomato or even an apple, or a celery knob or a scooped-out zucchini, or maybe even a nuclear reactor—now there's an apple a day that would keep everything away.

Apple Stuffing

Combine in a big bowl: two cored chopped apples, one small chopped onion, one egg, four tablespoons of melted butter, the juice of one lemon, one cup of sour cream, one tablespoon of chicken bouillon, and a quarter cup of white vermouth. Season with garlic, black pepper, and allspice; add enough bread crumbs to make it hold together as a stuffing should. Stuff something, heat, and eat.

Barbecue sauces, like fruit stuffings, are an easy way to liven up a fast meal. And they are not limited to grilling—use them anytime you prepare a quick-to-cook cutlet or fillet, whether it be meat, poultry, or fish. These two were for the picnic show on "Good Day! Live." I set up a hibachi out in the studio's parking lot overlooking the infamous Route 128, "America's Technology Highway"—some picnic!

Kirsch and Brandy Barbecue Sauce

Combine in a blender on its slowest speed: one cup kirsch, one cup cherry preserves, one tablespoon of cinnamon, and one-fourth cup each of your favorite mustard, frozen orange concentrate, brandy, chopped onion or shallots, and melted butter. This sauce is not only good for barbecuing chicken, pork, and lamb, but it's nice to use indoors on baked ham, duck, or any poultry. Makes just over three cups.

**Sambuca
Barbecue Sauce**

Whisk together a cup of melted butter, a cup of chopped shallots (or scallions, leeks, or onions), the juice of two lemons, four tablespoons of Sambuca, a tablespoon of chicken bouillon, and one teaspoon each of basil, black pepper, garlic, marjoram, nutmeg, parsley, savory, and thyme. This sauce also works beautifully on snails baked in a ramekin or as an artichoke dip. Makes nearly three cups.

No one should have to wait to eat a pizza like you do when you call up for one to go—"That'll be twenty minutes, please." This one's gone by then.

**Two-and-a-Half-
Minute Skillet Pizza**

Start with a low, round loaf of bread. Its diameter should closely match the frying pan you'll use. Cut the bread in half so that you have two round loaves (you'll love this pizza so much that you'll want to make another right away). Heat one-quarter inch of olive oil in the frying pan until it just begins to smoke. Quickly sprinkle in a healthy mixture of herbs—I use two tablespoons each of basil, black pepper, garlic, marjoram, oregano, and rosemary; also one tablespoon of beef bouillon. Add one cup of tomato sauce; stir a few times as it begins to bubble. Then sprinkle two cups of mixed grated provolone and Jarlsberg cheese and one-half cup of grated Parmesan evenly across the sauce. Lay the bread, cut side down, into the sauce. Let it simmer for about thirty seconds. Turn it upside down onto a plate and cut into wedges to serve. It goes without saying that you can add whatever you want to that sauce—mushrooms, pepperoni, and so on.

This next recipe is not a "cheesecake" as in the one-word spelling, but it is a super cheesy cake that's easily made in a frying pan like all upside-down cakes; I think the handle just makes it easier to flip onto a serving plate. Serve it hot or cold. With some greens, it's a meal in itself.

Upside-Down Tomato Cheese Cake

Butter the bottom of a twelve-inch ovenproof fry pan and line it with an arrangement of sliced cherry tomatoes. Season the tomatoes with any herb or spice of your choice—garlic, oregano, and tarragon are all good, as are nutmeg or curry. Pour the cake batter over the tomatoes and bake at 350° for thirty-five to forty minutes.

Cake Batter: Dump into a blender and whir until smooth: four eggs, one and a quarter cups of dry sherry (or white wine or milk), two cups of all-purpose flour, one and a half cups of grated cheese of your choice, two tablespoons of grated Parmesan, and three and a half teaspoons of baking powder. Season with white pepper.

Tomato Custard

Chop four large tomatoes into a blender. Add four eggs, one cup of light cream, one cup of sugar, and half a teaspoon each of salt and nutmeg. Blend until smooth. Butter a baking dish large enough to hold this mixture; pour in the tomato custard. Set the baking dish into a larger pan of hot water and bake uncovered at 350° for almost an hour. Remove from oven and let cool. Top with whipped cream and serve.

Tomatoes Baked in Herbs and Cheese

Slice off tomato tops and line up the tomatoes in a baking dish. Mix four tablespoons of melted butter with half a cup of red or white wine and pour over the tomatoes. Sprinkle with basil, dill, salt, and pepper; top with grated cheese—Swiss, Cheddar, and mozzarella work best. Bake uncovered at 400° for about thirty minutes. Serve while it's still sizzling.

Tomatoes Baked in Orange with Tarragon and Anisette

Set tomatoes in a baking dish (slice the tops off first). Mix half a cup of frozen orange concentrate with four tablespoons of melted butter, two shots of anisette, and some salt and pepper. Pour this over the tomatoes and bake uncovered at 400° for about thirty minutes. Serve hot from the oven.

Fried Green Tomatoes

Slice green tomatoes about a quarter-inch thick. Dip them first in beaten egg and then in bread crumbs. Fry the slices on each side in half an inch of sizzling butter or oil. Season with salt and pepper.

The preceding tomato dishes can each be served either as a small, quick meal by itself or in combination with another fast food from this chapter. Parsnips, a more substantial food than tomatoes, can certainly serve as meals in themselves. These roots are at their sweetest in the springtime, after having sat in the frozen earth all winter. Don't peel them, just brush them when you wash them. Some of the best and sweetest taste comes from the peelings. Carrots or sweet potatoes could replace the parsnips in the following three recipes, all solutions to leftover cooked vegetables.

Tugboat Parsnips

Combine two cups of mashed cooked parsnips with one tablespoon of butter, two egg yolks, and one tablespoon of flour. Season with salt and pepper. Shape into four to six flat cakes. Dip the cakes into cracker crumbs and fry in butter. Great for breakfast.

Shaker Parsnip Cakes

Fill the bottom of a bake-and-serve dish with halved cooked parsnips. Salt, pepper, and spice them as you'd like. Combine in a blender: two cups of sour cream, one-fourth cup of butter, four shots of dry sherry, one shot of Madeira, two tablespoons of flour, one tablespoon of thyme, and a couple of cooked parsnip halves. Blend smooth and season with salt, white pepper, garlic, and paprika. Arrange whole mushrooms among the parsnips, pour the sauce over, sprinkle with grated cheese of your choice and bake covered at 400° for twenty minutes. Or, start with raw parsnip halves, and bake about ten minutes longer.

(Shaker Parsnip Cakes)

Mix a cup of mashed cooked parsnips into an eight-ounce package of softened cream cheese. Blend in one-third cup of honey, a teaspoon of cinnamon, and the juice of half a lemon. Chill if desired; use as a spread on crackers or toast.

Parsnip "Butter"

Mix in a blender: three eggs, two cups water, and one cup each of cold water and ice. Dip asparagus spears into the blender, then slide them into hot deep fat. When golden brown, drain on paper. Serve sprinkled with orange juice, salt, and pepper.

Dipped Asparagus

Fast desserts always please my television viewers, not to mention the production crew who get to try them out for themselves without even writing in for the recipes. The first two desserts are from my "Apples Dearie" collection, named for that brilliant line in Snow White when the witch sticks her hand in the window, thrusting an apple at Snow White and cackling, "Apple, dearie?"

Core apples and slice into rings. Dip first in egg yolk, then in bread crumbs. Fry in hot oil. Drain; sprinkle with powdered sugar. Also good accompanying sausages; sprinkle with salt, pepper, curry powder, and sugar.

Fried Apple Rings

Blend a quarter cup each of melted butter and apricot brandy with a half cup each of raspberry preserves and orange concentrate. Pour over cored apples in a baking dish. Top with brown sugar and bake at 400° for thirty minutes.

Baked Apples in Raspberry-Orange Sauce with Apricot Brandy

The annual Strawberry Festival of South Berwick, Maine is held on the last Saturday in June. The first one was held two hundred years ago; the tradition was dropped somewhere along the way and only revived about ten years ago. I always sell dishes of strawberries with sour cream and brown sugar. The proceeds go to a good cause, the South Berwick Emergency Rescue Squad. In honor of that day, I created this recipe for a "Good Day! Live" appearance.

Deep South Berwick Strawberries

Whisk together a batter of three eggs, two cups of flour, three-fourths cup of maple syrup, four teaspoons of baking powder, and a dash of salt. Dip whole strawberries into the batter; fry in hot deep fat for only two minutes. Drain and sprinkle with lemon juice and powdered sugar.

Tomes have been written about tofu and its great value as a protein-laden meat substitute. I use it once in a while. It does blend well, acting as a healthy thickener in creamy desserts.

Tofu-Fruit Pudding

To one square of tofu in a blender, add one cup of any fresh fruit, the juice of one lemon, and about half a cup or more of honey. Your own taste is the best judge of the sweetness. Blend until smooth, pour into serving dishes, and let chill before serving. Recommended fruit includes rhubarb, sour cherries, mango, and papaya.

Tofu Mousse

Blend two squares of tofu with four egg yolks, about three-fourths cup of honey, any flavoring (such as a melted square of chocolate, a cup of fruit, or a couple of spoonfuls of vanilla extract), and a good shot of some corresponding brandy. When smooth, pour it into a saucepan and warm over a low heat until it begins to simmer. Stir until the mixture becomes thick

and custardy. Run through the blender once more. **(Tofu Mousse)**
Whip up the four egg whites and gently fold them into
the custard. Pour into champagne glasses and let cool.

Chocolate truffles get their name from their resemblance to the
fungi. The original recipe calls for four ounces of bitter chocolate
to be melted down with a tablespoon of milk and beaten with two
tablespoons of butter and one egg yolk. It is then left to harden,
made into little stick shapes, and rolled in powdered chocolate.

Cream a half cup of butter with a tablespoon of sugar, **Chocolate Truffle**
then add two and a half tablespoons of cocoa powder **Cake**
and one tablespoon of corn syrup (or flavored brandy).
Press this into a greased bottomless six-inch cake pan
or flan ring placed on a cookie sheet. Chill until firm.
Remove the pan or ring and roll the "cake" in
chopped nuts to coat the side. Melt two ounces of milk
chocolate with two teaspoons of water or brandy in
a bowl set over hot water or in a double boiler; pour
over cake. Decorate with whatever strikes your fancy.
Serve warm or chilled.

Sauces for a Crowd

There is that rare occasion for all of us when we are faced with the horror of cooking for a large crowd—a wedding, christening, graduation, or, of course, a funeral. It's the day that our mother, grandmothers, and aunts arrive with that incredible look on their faces that says, "How can you possibly do anything right, let alone cook for forty people?" (Aren't parents amazing? To this day my mother drags up the story about the time I put six bulbs, instead of cloves, of garlic into a spaghetti sauce when I was fifteen.) So, whether you're throwing a party or hosting a family gathering, you're sure to find something in this chapter of crowd (and mother) pleasers.

The proportions for such cooking are really very simple. "A quarter of a pound of each course will feed one person." If you had gone to culinary school, that last line would have cost you about eight hundred dollars and lots of boring hours. All of the sauce recipes here will yield five to seven cups, enough for ten pounds of anything. If you are doing a meal for forty people, ten pounds of each dish will suffice. I hate telling you what foods to serve with which sauces, so mix and match to your heart's content!

I like to choose foods that can be baked; the cooking times are easily organized, freeing you from peeking and poking under pan lids. You can prepare a quantity of sauce ahead and clean, slice, season, and arrange the raw foods in baking dishes. The cooking is simple. Pour the sauce over, cover, and place in a 400° oven—staggering the start time of each course. Green vegetables will take forty minutes for ten pounds while more substantial vegetables (carrots, potatoes, and winter squashes) should cook for an hour and a half. Whole birds and veal roasts usually take twenty to twenty-five minutes per pound, while ten pounds of individual servings in a baking pan should take anywhere from sixty to ninety minutes, depending on the size of each piece. Little chicken wings obviously would fall on the low side of that scale; the longer time is more for thick, stuffed chops and the like. Got the idea? Pork should cook for a long time and be served well done. That translates to thirty-five minutes a pound for roasts, and about two hours total for ten pounds of individual servings. For good beef such as tenderloin, turn the heat up to 500° and allow ten minutes per pound to roast a whole tenderloin or ten to fifteen minutes total to bake ten pounds of individual servings such as sauced medallions. All fish, if not greater than two inches thick, can be cooked in twelve to fifteen minutes, also at 500°; this includes stuffed and rolled fillets. Are you still with me?

I've begun with two examples of a truly versatile type of sauce, the indoor-outdoor "barbecue" sauce. Included in the "Fast Food" chapter are two others, yielding only three cups each—Kirsch and Brandy Barbecue Sauce and Sambuca Barbecue Sauce.

Barbecue Sauce with Tomato, Southern Comfort, and Maple

You're off to an easy start with a quart of prepared barbecue sauce; that way you get the benefit of its pineapple vinegar. Otherwise, simply combine equal parts of catsup and tomato sauce and then work from there. To a quart of "sauce," add one-half cup each of

**(Barbecue Sauce
with Tomato,
Southern Comfort,
and Maple)**

Southern Comfort, maple syrup, and vinegar (red wine is best, but white or cider vinegar will do). Season with a quarter cup of minced onion, the juice of two lemons, two tablespoons crushed and chopped garlic (or two of powder), and one tablespoon each of basil, ginger, and black pepper. Combine all the ingredients well. Be generous when pouring over cooking beef, hamburgers, or pork. It's even nice on vegetables, fish, and chicken.

**Peach Brandy
Barbecue Sauce**

Blend two cups of peach brandy and one-half cup of peach preserves with one and a third cups of frozen orange concentrate, one and a half cups of vinegar, one-fourth cup of flour, four cloves of garlic, two tablespoons each of hot mustard, Worcestershire sauce, and A-1 sauce, three drops of Tabasco, and two shakes of white pepper. This is delightful baked over frog legs.

The next six sauces are based on wine, vermouth, cognac, or sherry. You could easily transform any one of them into a "Champagne Sauce." Champagne is not such an expensive and exotic liquid with which to cook. There are some inexpensive American champagnes that are just fine for cooking. There is also a Spanish champagne on the market that is excellent for drinking and simply grand for cooking. What do you do with a champagne sauce? For starters, try Turkey Breast in a Champagne Cream Sauce with Crabmeat (page 54), Roast Leg of Veal in a Champagne and Bacon Cream Sauce (page 61), or Quail with Walnut Cheese and Smoked Mussels in a Champagne and Lobster Sauce (page 51).

Another fun way to please a crowd is to serve a dish with a flaming sauce. Baby Beef Wellingtons (page 64) are served in this manner with Mushroom Cognac Sauce. Try it with any cognac or brandy sauce; just be sure you have insurance.

In a blender combine a cup and a half of honey, one and a half bottles of Cold Duck, three or four chopped apples, and cinnamon and white pepper to taste. Add enough chicken bouillon to cut the sweetness, but not to taste salty.

Honey and Cold Duck Glaze

This is highly recommended for salmon. Blend one cup of melted butter with a handful of chopped shallots, four cups each of heavy and sour cream, one cup of white wine, one-half cup of flour, one-third cup of paprika, the juice of two lemons, two tablespoons of chicken bouillon, and some garlic and white pepper to taste. Pour into a saucepan and simmer until thick, stirring often. Also good with lamb or cauliflower.

White Wine and Sour Cream Paprika Sauce

A simpler white wine sauce is White Wine Parsley Sauce (page 40), which I serve with haddock and langostinos. Vermouth, which is an herbed and spiced white wine, obviously is just the thing for wine sauces. Try my White Vermouth Cream Sauce, described with the recipe for Veal Cutlet Stuffed with Artichoke and Pimiento (page 68). If you'd rather not have a cream sauce, try this next tomato-based one with mushrooms. I like it on snails, but you could use it on baked oysters, clams, or mussels; also on cubed swordfish or shark, and even on mushrooms or cauliflower.

Pour two cups of melted butter into a blender. Add four whole tomatoes, one chopped large onion, one cup of vermouth, and the juice of two lemons. Add two tablespoons of chicken bouillon, one tablespoon of basil, six or so large mushrooms, a handful of chopped parsley, and black pepper and garlic to taste. Chop on the lowest speed; sauce should have some lumps.

Vermouth-Mushroom Sauce

Cognac and Leek Sauce

Brown a handful of chopped shallots in a melted stick of butter. Add one-half cup of flour and let that brown lightly, stirring often. Remove from heat and set aside. Blend one and a half cups of heavy cream and half a cup of cognac with one-half cup of chopped onions, a tablespoon of frozen orange concentrate, a tomato (or some catsup or both), a sprinkling of savory, a drizzle of honey, and a taste of chicken bouillon. Then add the butter and shallot mixture from the pan. Blend again. Return the smoothened sauce to the pot; add three bunches of chopped leeks and two cups of red wine. Simmer until thick. Best with red meats.

Plum and Cinnamon Port Wine Sauce

Melt one cup of butter in a saucepan. Add one cup of plum jam, two cups of port wine, one-half cup of frozen orange concentrate, and two tablespoons of cinnamon. Simmer, stirring frequently, for about thirty minutes. This sauce is good for carrots, yellow squashes, game, lamb, pork, rabbit, and birds; I don't recommend it with beef.

Sherried Crabmeat Sauce

Brown a handful of chopped shallots in a cup of hot butter. Stir in one-half cup of flour. Then add three cups of heavy cream, a cup of dry sherry, one-half cup of port wine, two tablespoons of chicken bouillon, and the juice of two lemons. Sprinkle with white pepper, garlic, and parsley. Simmer, stirring often, until thick. Finally, fold in two pounds of crabmeat and keep the sauce on low heat just long enough for the crabmeat to warm through.

Sometimes just a simple butter sauce will suffice. For instance, when I bake a pan of potatoes, I like to bathe them in the following wine and butter mixture. Other wines and spirits blend as well with butter, and using one of "Your Own Butters" (pages 5-9) couldn't hurt. Maybe Beef Tenderloin in Filo with Shrimp and Artichoke Stuffing in a Lemon Butter Cognac Sauce (page 59) will inspire you to create your own simple butter sauces.

Simple Butter Sauce with Wine

Melt two cups of butter in a large saucepan. Add two diced large onions, two cups of white wine, four tablespoons of chicken bouillon, two tablespoons of chopped garlic, two handfuls of snipped chives, and black pepper to taste. Simmer, stirring frequently, for about fifteen minutes. I usually pour this over ten pounds of sliced potatoes and bake at 400° for ninety minutes.

Some dishes call for a cold sauce, such as Cold Salmon in an Orange Custard Sauce (page 43) or Lobster Salad in Sambuca and Bacon Sour Cream (page 43). Here is a citrus-flavored mayonnaise with bacon to use perhaps on chicken salad, a Nicoise-style salad, mussels, or any fish.

Orange and Bacon Mayonnaise

Crisp-fry, then crumble, a pound of bacon. Throw it into a blender with four cups of homemade or prepared mayonnaise, and six tablespoons each of frozen orange concentrate and lime juice. Blend well.

Mayonnaise sauces don't have to be served cold. I serve a Hot Sambuca Mayonnaise with Chicken Stir-Fry with Raisins (page 48). Some sauces are good hot or cold, and some soups are potential sauces. When chilled, Herb and May Wine Summer Cream Soup (page 23) would toss well with potato salad. Creamy salad dressings can serve as sauces, too. Black Olive and Sour Cream Dressing and Pimiento Sour Cream Dressing are both found at the end of the salad chapter; consider Curried Maple Syrup Dressing or

Strawberry and Honey Dressing also. And don't forget pestos (page 37).

On the sweeter side, here are two fruit "sauces" that also make great gifts when nicely bottled. Following the chutney and brandied fruit recipes are three ideas for what I call "dessert pesto." All five recipes yield generous amounts.

Cranberry Chutney American Style   Boil one pound of cranberries with two cups of Southern Comfort, two cups of orange juice, one cup of maple syrup, one cup of catsup, a half cup of vinegar, two medium chopped green tomatoes, one cup each of walnut halves and chopped fresh pineapple, a half cup of chopped raw parsnips, and some black pepper to taste. Reduce heat and simmer until reduced by a third. Pour into a jar and refrigerate. Good on cold (or hot) meats, birds, and smoked fish.

Brandied Winter Fruit   In a baking pan spread a pound each of pitted dried apricots, currants, dates, figs, pecans, and prunes. Mix in cubes of fresh fruit—a pound of pears, six apples, and one pineapple. Bathe in sauce, cover tightly, and bake at 400° for almost an hour.

Sauce: Blend four cups of creme de cassis, two cups brandy, and one cup maple syrup. Add salt, pepper, and basil to taste.

"Brandied Winter Fruit" can be used as a sauce, a dessert, or an accompaniment to wild game. Jar and save it; serve it cold. If you add two cups of diced leftover pork, goose, or turkey, you'll have mincemeat for a special pie. Try it atop baked apples or pears, too.

Chocolate isn't entirely awful for you. It's mostly what you mix into it that makes it so bad, usually too much sugar and fat. Of course, the caffeine is no great help either. I learned once that 250 milligrams of caffeine can neutralize vitamins in your body and may also interfere with certain medications. Think about that the next time you bring a box of chocolates to a friend in the hospital. But as long as you're not a heavy coffee drinker or chocolate fanatic, these "pestos" will actually be good for you—in small doses, please; it's concentrated stuff.

Chocolate Pesto

Melt four ounces of baking chocolate with one cup of Frangelico, two cups of honey, and two tablespoons of vanilla. Bring this to a boil; then simmer for about fifteen minutes, stirring constantly. Meanwhile in the food processor, chop three-fourths cup each of dried currants, dried apricots, and dates; one-half cup each of Brazil nuts, walnuts, and filberts; and one cup of grated coconut. The processing should take thirty to forty-five seconds. Add the hot chocolate mixture and process another thirty seconds. Heap immediately onto vanilla ice cream, peach sherbet, or pound or angel food cake.

White Chocolate Pesto

Melt two cups of broken white chocolate pieces, add one cup of Grand Marnier or Drambuie, bring to a boil, and then simmer for about fifteen minutes. Combine with the same processed fruits and nuts as in the preceding recipe Or, you might want to add a fruity brandy and just use coconut, or all filberts and a chocolate mint liqueur.

Butterscotch Pesto

Heat a base sauce of one cup Amaretto, two cups brown sugar, four tablespoons of vanilla, and the juice of one lemon. Boil and simmer as above, and mix into whatever combination of processed fruits and nuts you'd like.

I could go on for days sharing with you my ideas for sauces for a crowd. Don't you stop with this chapter. Perusing the meat, fish, and birds chapters, you'll find ideas for a peanut butter sauce, a cucumber sauce, a blueberry and crème de cassis sauce, a curried tomato Grand Marnier sour cream sauce, a lemon pimiento Pernod sauce, a walnut cheese sauce, and many others. Start a book of your own sauces, why don't you?

After Dinner

Fruit—eat fruit after dinner. Dip strawberries in sour cream and brown sugar. That's the most sensible thing for after dinner; it's been my standby for years in the restaurant. But once in a while, there is that "occasion" that calls for something big, rich, creamy, and sweet. And anything that fills that description is "dessert." Of course, what comes to mind immediately is cheesecake.

CHEESECAKE

About a year ago, I discovered I could make cheesecake. The world—and my physique—has not been the same since. I make praline cheesecakes, praline chocolate cheesecakes, also Nesselrode, almond, and chocolate nougat cheesecakes—and all of them generously laced with luscious liqueurs. The only problem is that I make big ones; you could probably slice eighteen to twenty servings from one of my cakes. But cheesecake should be made large—it's too nice not to have around to share. It's also a kind of special event to make a cheesecake. (I hate the word "special." Those same people who ruined words like "gourmet," "viable," and "agenda" have ruined "special." I am always cautious about meeting people who are referred to as "special.")

There's a formula for cheesecake. It's simple, quick, and only on occasion is it expensive.

Combine one and a half pounds of cream cheese, four eggs, one cup of flavoring (not concentrated, unless frozen orange juice), one cup of liqueur, one cup of "sugar," and four tablespoons of flour. I generally do this in a blender or a food processor. And that's it. The formula for some varieties changes a bit, but not enough to make it frightening.

Once your batter is established, you'll need a crumb crust to compliment the cake. The first time I did Chocolate Nougat Cheesecake with Frangelico, I used Amaretto di Sarrono cookies and that crust cost me nine dollars. You could achieve a perfectly lovely effect by using graham crackers, butter, and chocolate powder. But try this. Throw a half box of any kind of cookies into a processor. Add two-thirds of a stick of butter and two tablespoons of unsweetened cocoa powder. Using the chopper blade, process long enough to completely mix the crumbs with the butter. Set aside a spoonful or so of the mixture (to sprinkle later on top of the cake, not to snack on) and press the rest onto the floor and sides of a large (twelve-inch) buttered springform pan. (If you don't have a springform pan, use a foil collar to build up the side of any cake or pie pan. Press the crumbs only up to the top of the pan; the filling can be higher. Gently pull the foil away after the cake is cooked.)

Pour in your cream cheese concoction. Bake at 400° for fifteen minutes; reduce heat to 225° and bake for another hour and a half (more or less). Chill overnight for best results or go ahead and eat it as soon as it's cold.

There are also "pastes" that are available at some specialty stores such as almond paste, praline paste, and Nesselrode. If you know where to shop and what you're looking for, you'll discover lots of "candy" that can be turned into lots of desserts. Don't neglect the possibilities of my dessert "pestos" (page 101) either.

Chocolate Nougat Cheesecake with Frangelico

Combine one and a half pounds of cream cheese with four eggs, six Tobler milk chocolate bars, one cup of Frangelico, and six tablespoons of flour. The candy bars provide both the flavoring and the sugar here. Create a crumb crust and pour in the cake mixture. Bake as suggested in the preceding basic formula.

White Chocolate Cheesecake with Raspberries and Crème de Cassis

You might want to use vanilla wafers in the crust for this one since the cheese mixture tends to taste of vanilla; I think it's nice to carry that through the whole cake. As usual, start with one and a half pounds of cream cheese. Blend the cheese thoroughly with four eggs, a cup of white chocolate pieces, a half cup of Bailey's Irish Cream, four tablespoons of flour, half a cup of vanilla sugar, and four tablespoons of vanilla extract. Pour into a crumb crust and bake as suggested in the basic formula recipe. Top the cooled cooked cake with raspberries and warm crème de cassis "syrup" —prepared by simmering one and a half cups crème de cassis until it's reduced by half.

Butterbrickle Cheesecake à la Ippolito

It's as easy to make as it sounds. Crush two cups of chocolate-covered butterbrickle. If you do it in a food processor, don't let it get mushy—it works best if the candy is ice cold or even frozen. Set aside. Using the food processor again (or a blender), mix a pound and a half of cream cheese with four eggs, one cup of Irish cream liqueur, and a quarter cup of flour. When smooth, pour the cheese mixture over the butterbrickle and combine well. Pour into a prepared crumb

(Butterbrickle Cheesecake)

crust in a large springform pan. Bake at 450° for ten minutes, then at 225° for about ninety minutes. Chill a long time, even overnight.

Cointreau Cheesecake with Candied Orange Slices

Again, prepare a crumb crust for a large ten- to twelve-inch springform pan. Using the chopping blade in your processor, combine one and a half pounds of cream cheese with six eggs, one cup of frozen orange concentrate, half a cup of Cointreau, a quarter cup of honey, four tablespoons of flour, and two tablespoons of grated orange rind. Pour into your crumb crust and bake as directed in the preceding recipe. Chill, then top with candied orange.

Candied Orange Slices: Slice two unpeeled, seedless oranges as thin as you can; lay them aside. In a small pan, heat one cup of Cointreau with one cup of white sugar. Boil this mixture, stirring often, until it is reduced to a syrup. Add the orange slices and simmer them in the syrup until they soften, about fifteen minutes. Arrange these candied fruit slices on top of the cooled cheesecake. Chill completely before serving. Or, for a fancy occasion; raise the heat under the candied fruit, add a cup of Drambuie, and ignite. Pour, flaming, over servings of cheesecake.

Now, if you're looking for a quickie—you're suddenly faced with entertaining someone "special" (I told you to watch out for those kind) or you're in the middle of a cheesecake "attack,"—then try a cheesecake pudding. If you have a food processor, these are made in about five minutes. You can do them as well by hand, but it will take a little longer.

Cheesecake Pudding

Melt sixteen ounces of cream cheese in a saucepan. Blend in four eggs and cook over low heat until the whole mixture bubbles. Pour it into a food processor and add another pound of cream cheese and one cup of any "sweet sauce" you like. For instance, add two candy bars, and it's a Toffee and Chocolate Cheesecake Pudding. Use one cup of any kind of preserves—cherry, Nesselrode, mincemeat, orange or lemon marmalade—and name it accordingly. In any case, process until the mixture is super-smooth and creamy. Fill parfait dishes or glasses and top with a hint of whatever you mixed into it. Good chilled.

(Cheesecake Pudding)

Like the basic Cheesecake Pudding, this rich ricotta cake is unbaked, although it is simmered to thicken. It can also be served in parfait dishes or attractive glasses or in a crust.

Brandied Pear Cheesecake

Combine in a blender: one cup of ricotta cheese, one eight-ounce package of cream cheese, four egg yolks, one cup of sugar, the juice of one lemon, and two sliced pears. Blend until smooth and pour into a saucepan. Simmer until thick, stirring frequently. Pour into a prepared crust of your choice or into individual glasses or dishes. Let set. Top with brandied pears and chill.

Brandied Pears: Cut two pears into halves; remove core and seeds. Simmer in one cup of brandy for about ten minutes. When cool enough to handle, thin-slice halves crosswise. Arrange on top of cheesecake and drizzle with any excess brandy.

This next recipe, an inspiration of friends, takes cheesecake one step beyond the basic batter into the realm of mousse. It is thickened with gelatin, rich with whipped cream, and lightened with egg whites. The crust is a gem.

Pumpkin Rosamond in a Gardino Crust

In a blender, combine one cup of prepared pumpkin, three egg yolks (you'll use the whites later), eight

(Pumpkin Rosamond in a Gardino Crust)

ounces of cream cheese, one cup of powdered sugar, one tablespoon of cinnamon, the juice of one lemon, a quarter cup of liqueur (Cointreau, Amaretto, Tia Maria, Grand Marnier, or whatever), and two envelopes of gelatin. Blend until smooth; transfer to a saucepan. Stirring, simmer until mixture becomes thick and custardy. Blend again and set aside to cool at room temperature. While the custard is cooling, prepare crust and line a springform pan with the mixture (set a few spoonfuls aside). Then pour a third of the cooled pumpkin into the pan. Whip a half-pint of heavy cream and fold it into another third of the pumpkin custard. Lay that atop the first layer. Fold the remaining pumpkin into three stiff-beaten egg whites. Spread that across the second layer. Sprinkle remaining cookie crumbs on top and set cake in the refrigerator until ice cold. Unmold and serve.

Crust: Crush one package each of Bordeaux cookies and Molasses Crisps into crumbs and mix them into four tablespoons of melted butter.

PIE

Some would call Pumpkin Rosamond in a Gardino Crust a pie. Though not in the same class as cheesecake, pies generally do meet all the criteria for dessert—big, rich, creamy and sweet. The following custard meringue pie could be made with fruit other than pears. Try it with kiwi, peaches, or cherries; vary the juice and spice in the custard base, too. The second pie I've chosen to share with you was inspired by the Shakers' thrifty use of homegrown produce. Tomato Pie is a terrific solution to an over-abundant crop; this dessert is also wholesome and certainly novel.

Prepare a butter crust (page 104) and line a pie pan with it. Brush the inside of the crust with the following glaze: a quarter cup of orange marmalade (or any jam or jelly) blended with a shot of brandy (or liqueur of your choice). You shouldn't have to use all of this glaze; save some to flavor the meringue later. Quarter, core, and seed two pears; lay them in the bottom. Pour the custard mixture over the pears and bake at 400° for ten minutes. Reduce heat to 325° and bake for another thirty-five minutes. Top with dollops of meringue and bake again at 400° until the meringue lightly browns.

Custard: Thoroughly combine six egg yolks, four egg whites, a cup of sugar, a cup of melted butter, the juice of one lemon, and a teaspoon of ground ginger.

Meringue: Beat two egg whites until soft peaks form. Fold the remaining brandy glaze into the beaten egg whites.

Pear Custard Meringue Pie

Peel four to six ripe tomatoes, slice, and sprinkle a little salt over them. Let the salted slices sit for about twenty minutes, then drain the accumulated juice. Line a pie plate with your favorite crust and fill with drained tomatoes. Cover with a mixture of half a cup of heavy cream, one egg, a tablespoon of cinnamon, and about three-fourths cup of sugar. Top with another layer of crust and bake in a 350° oven for about thirty minutes.

Tomato Pie

CAKE

On those evenings when only a chocolate cake will do for after dinner, I've just the one for you. My grandma's devil's food cake with walnuts and coffee icing is one of the fondest memories of my childhood. Actually, there are three distinct wonderful times associated with that cake—licking the bowl, biting into the first piece, and scooping up the leftover crumbs and bits of icing stuck to the cake platter. My grandma had always promised to give me the recipe, but alas, she slipped away one Easter morning, and for twenty years I had only the memory of that cake. Then, a couple of years ago, my aunt found a letter that my grandma had sent her when she was first married—and there on the back page was this recipe. It's the original "pudding-in-a-box."

My Grandma's Devil's Food Cake

Cook this pudding first so it has time to cool while you prepare the batter. Melt four squares of unsweetened chocolate with five tablespoons each of sugar and milk and one tablespoon of flour. Stirring, simmer until thick and smooth like a pudding. Whisk in two tablespoons of vanilla, then remove from heat and let cool.

Batter: Cream together three-fourths of a cup of butter or shortening and one cup of sugar. Whisk in a dash of salt and two eggs. Gradually blend in one cup of buttermilk and two cups of flour (mixed with a teaspoon of baking soda). Beat until smooth, then add a cup of chopped walnuts. Fold in cooled pudding last. Butter and flour a tube pan (that's what my grandma liked to use), pour in cake mixture, and bake at 325° for one hour. Remove from pan to cool. Add icing of your choice. I like it dribbled with a coffee butter cream.

My grandmother and I had a real connection with food. She always tucked butterscotch Life Savers into the pocket of her black sealskin coat and she always "splurged" on a pound of black cherries for us to share—that and caramel corn were our treats. Born on Halloween in Pulaski, Wisconsin, she raised five children by herself and taught me to feel most at home in the kitchen. The day after her funeral, I bought a small bag of caramel corn and went out to lay it with the flowers on her grave. She was one woman who showed me true tenderness.

COFFEE

When I was a little boy, my mother showed me how to float heavy cream on top of black coffee—sliding it off a spoon that was ever-so-lightly sitting on the surface, just barely resting against the side of the cup. She called it "French coffee," and assured me that it was a certain test as to whether or not the cream you had been served was really cream—something that was before light cream, half and half, heavy cream, whipping cream, ultra-pasteurized, and whatever else they've come up with since. There was milk, and there was cream—that was it.

Coffee isn't even coffee anymore. Trendy shops are promoting flavored coffees which are great to have, but you needn't spend six dollars a pound for them. Perk up your own coffee—and your life—for half the price.

Chocolate Almond Coffee

Splash three pounds of coffee beans with an ounce and a half of chocolate extract. Let it dry, add a handful of chopped almonds, and grind it just as you'd grind normal coffee. I do about a fourth of the mixture at a time in a blender on the "grind" setting. Store it in a cold place.

If Chocolate Almond Coffee seems too pedestrian, to the same three pounds of beans, add an ounce and a half (a shot or two) of Vandermint, Amaretto, or Frangelico and throw in black walnuts, pecans, or filberts. If you topped them all with flavored whipped cream, the coffee could become the dessert itself.

Menus

This is so unlike me, to itemize what to serve with what! These are just suggestions for putting together six-course dinners like those we serve at the Blue Strawbery Restaurant. But nothing's sacred here. A green is a green, an entree is an entree. Make substitutions depending on what you have on hand and what you'd like to eat. All the recipes are in this book.

Herb and May Wine Summer Cream Soup
Goose Livers in Marmalade and Brandy Sauce
Dandelion Greens with Black Walnut Dressing
Striped Bass with Crabmeat in Cucumber Sauce
Shaker Parsnip Cakes
Tomatoes Baked in Orange with Tarragon and Anisette
Deep South Berwick Strawberries

Vatican Vichyssoise
Goose Liver Pâté
Pineapple and Red Cabbage Salad
Haddock in Plums and Brandy
Carrots in Frangelico and Coffee
Zucchini and Spinach with Nasturtiums
Tomato Pie

Beet Green–Buttermilk Chowder
Artichoke Hearts in Brie Custard
Zucchini and Grapefruit in Raspberry-Honey Dressing
Frogs' Legs in Lemon and Pimiento-Pernod Sauce
Fried Green Tomatoes
Curried Sweet Potato and Cranberry Swirl
Butterbrickle Cheesecake à la Ippolito

Baked Salmon Bisque
Goose Livers with Artichoke Hearts in a
Champagne and Bacon Sauce
Fresh Greens in Almond Sherry Vinegar
Breast of Duck in Cranberries and Crème de Cassis
Dandelion Greens with Black Walnut Dressing
Roast Potatoes in a Bacon Cream Sauce
Baked Tomatoes in Sambuca and Lemon Herb Butter
Strawberries with Sour Cream and Brown Sugar

Tomato Clam Broth with Shrimp and Nori
Mussels with Watercress, Macadamia Nut, and Jarlsberg Pesto
Sweet and Sour Apples, Bacon, and Zucchini
Shark Janis Paige
Cauliflower Crown
White Chocolate Pesto on Peach Sherbet

Chicken Claret with Casaba Melon
Rabbit Almondine in Mustard Maple Syrup
Peaches and Sliced Radishes in Orange–Juniper Berry Vinegar
Emerald City Salad
Lamb Stir-Fry with Scallions and Pears
Eggplant, Tomatoes, and Pine Nuts
Chocolate Nougat Cheesecake with Frangelico

Seafood in a Sherried Clam Broth
Snails in Peach Brandy Barbecue Sauce
Greens with Black Olive and Sour Cream Dressing
Veal Cutlets Stuffed with Apple in a Walnut-Cheese Sauce
Tomatoes Baked in Nutmeg and Basil Butter
Wild Rice with Mushrooms
Pumpkin Rosamond in a Gardino Crust

Smoked Mussels in Sherried Tomato Cream
Lobster and Havarti Cognac Cream Sauce on Fettucine
Melon with Raw Salmon in a Ginger Sauce
Chicken Stir-Fry with Raisins and Sambuca Mayonnaise
Spinach in Mint Butter
Tomatoes Baked in Curried Pear Butter
Baked Apples in Raspberry-Orange Sauce with Apricot Brandy

Cream of Wild Rice Soup
Mussels in a Peach Lobster Butter
Apples, Cucumbers, and Carrots with Curried Maple Syrup Dressing
Hot Mangoes Stuffed with Duck
Dandelion Greens and Cucumber
Tomatoes Baked in Herbs and Cheese
Strawberries with Sour Cream and Brown Sugar

Champagne and Radish Cream Soup
Cold Smoked Mussels in Sour Cream and Onions
Apple, Pineapple, and Cucumber Salad
Trout Stuffed with Romaine
Stuffed Celery Knobs
Baked Tomato in Orange Marmelade and Cointreau
Tofu Mousse

Peanut Butter and Orange Soup
Mussels with Curried Duxelles in Brandy Topping
Bacon, Yogurt, and Chives on Peaches and Crab Legs
Roast Pork with Cabbage, Potatoes, and Burgundy Sauerkraut
Fried Apple Rings
Butterscotch Pesto on Angel Food Cake

Sherried Mussel Cream Soup
Goose Liver Pâté
Greens with Raspberry Champagne Vinegar
Turkey Meltdown
Collard Greens with Lemon Butter
Cranberry Chutney American Style
Fresh Fruit

Cream of Radish Soup
Goose Livers in Marmalade and Brandy Sauce
Shredded White Radish and Sliced Orange
Beef Tenderloin Flambé in Bacon and Mushroom Brandy Sauce
Beet Green, Cashew, and Havarti Pesto on Fettucine
Tomatoes Baked in Lemon Sherry Butter
Strawberries with Sour Cream and Brown Sugar

Curried Asparagus Cream Soup
Mussels with Strawberry–Black Pepper Topping
Nasturtium Salad
Breast of Duck in Rhubarb and Crème de Cassis
Wild Rice
Baked Tomatoes in Sambuca and Lemon Herb Butter
Cointreau Cheesecake with Candied Orange Slices

Goose Livers in Cognac Cream Soup
Mussels with Sambuca Herb Butter
Cucumbers and Strawberries with Strawberry–Port Wine Vinegar
Tuna Steak in Olive Oil and Honey
Beet Greens
Celery Patties
Fried Apples
Chocolate Truffle Cake

Ina Zwicker's Whitehead Island Chowder
Artichoke Hearts in Havarti and Sherry Custard
Zucchini and Grapefruit in Raspberry-Honey Dressing
Crab-stuffed Sole in Tomato-Cognac Sauce
Fried Green Tomatoes
Zucchini and Spinach with Nasturtiums
Deep South Berwick Strawberries

Artichoke Heart and Corn Chowder
Conchs with Spinach-Garlic Stuffing
Nasturtium Salad
Baby Beef Wellingtons
Dipped Asparagus
Roast Potatoes in a Bacon Cream Sauce
Carrots in Ginger Ale
Strawberries with Sour Cream and Brown Sugar

Cream of Fiddlehead Fern Soup
Rabbit in Orange Barbecue Sauce
Romaine with Lemon-Pepper Vinegar
Fillet of Sole with Mussels in Sherry Butter
Roast Potatoes in a Bacon Cream Sauce
Sweet and Sour Fried Green Tomatoes
Carrots in Root Beer
Strawberries with Sour Cream and Brown Sugar

Epilogue

To my students
Albert Boulanger, Burton Richardson, Ray McCracken,
Mark Gardino, Daniel Sturtevant, Philip McGuire,
and Jeffrey Plowman

Pot, pot, o wondrous pot,
O kettle boiling dreams,
the fire is there
and the moon is fair
and nothing is as it seems.
Boil, perk, and simmer too;
therein the answer steams.
For only where
the fearless dare
is the land of answered dreams.
Cook and stir and fricassee;
add all your day-old schemes.
For when you dare
the sweet dish of care,
you'll find your fondest dreams.

Index

Almond-Sherry Vinegar, 36
Apple(s):
  baked, in raspberry-orange sauce with apricot brandy, 91
  and parsnips, with roast stuffed pork, 64–65
  rings, fried, 91
  salad, with pineapple and cucumber, 31
  Stuffing, 87
  sweet and sour, with bacon and zucchini, 31
  in veal cutlets, with a walnut-cheese sauce, 67
Artichoke heart(s):
  in Brie Custard, 11
  and Corn Chowder, 22
  with creamed lobster, 43
  with goose livers in a champagne and bacon sauce, 13–14
  in Havarti and Sherry Custard, 11
  and pimiento, with stuffed veal cutlets, 67–68
  with salmon, in orange-lobster cream, 42–43
  and shrimp stuffing, 59
Asparagus:
  cream soup, curried, 24
  dipped, 91

Baby Beef Wellingtons, 57–58, 96
Bacon:
  and champagne cream sauce, 61–62
  and collards, in stuffed sweet potatoes, 75
  cream sauce, for roast potatoes, 76–77
  and Mushroom Brandy Sauce, 59–60
  and onions, with sweet and sour carrots, 72
  and orange mayonnaise, 99
  in salad, with sweet and sour apples and zucchini, 31
  and Sambuca sour cream, for lobster-orange salad, 43–44
  and spinach cognac Caesar, 33
  Yogurt, and Chives on Peaches and Crab Legs, 32
Baked Apples in Raspberry-Orange Sauce with Apricot Brandy, 91
Baked Salmon Bisque, 21
Baked Tomatoes in Orange Marmalade and Cointreau, 74
Baked Tomatoes in Sambuca and Lemon Herb Butter, 74
Baking time, estimating, 95

Barbecue Sauce(s):
  Kirsch and Brandy, 87
  Peach Brandy, 96
  Sambuca, 88
  with Tomato, Southern Comfort, and Maple, 95–96
Basil and nutmeg butter, 8
Bass, striped:
  in a cognac-sour cream sauce with scallops, 40–41
  with crabmeat in cucumber sauce, 41
Beef:
  Tenderloin in Filo with Shrimp and Artichoke Stuffing, 58–59, 99
  Tenderloin Flambe in Bacon and Mushroom Brandy Sauce, 59–60
  tenderloin pate, sweet and sour, in filo, 58
  Tenderloin in a Peanut Butter Sauce, 60
  Wellingtons, Baby, 57–58
Beet Green(s), 71
  and buttermilk chowder, 22–23
  Cashew, and Havarti Pesto, 83
  pesto, with brie, for chicken breast, 47
  with tuna roast, 39
Bisque. *See* Soup
Blackberries in fresh butter, 6

Black Olive and Sour Cream Dressing, 37, 99
Blueberry and Creme de Cassis Sauce, 49, 102
Boned Quail in a Crown of Lobster Pate, 52
Brandied Pear Cheesecake, 107
Brandied Winter Fruit, 100
Breast of Duck:
  in Blueberries and Creme de Cassis, 49
  in Cranberries and Creme de Cassis, 49
  in Grape Leaves with Grapefruit, 50
  in Rhubarb and Creme de Cassis, 50
Broth:
  Sherried Clam, for seafood, 28–29
  Tomato Clam, with shrimp and nori, 29
Butter:
  Cinnamon Orange, 8
  Curried Pear, 8
  Fruit-flavored, 8
  Garlic, Supreme, 8
  herbed, 8–9
  with liqueur, 8–9
  making your own, 5–9
  Mint, 8
  Nasturtium, 7
  Nutmeg and Basil, 8
  nutritional value of, 6
  Parsnip, 91
  Peach Lobster, 15–16
  Sambuca Herb, 15
  Sambuca and lemon herb, for baked tomatoes, 74
  sherry, 42
  sweet, 8–9
  Sweet Curry, 7–8
Butterbrickle Cheesecake a la Ippolito, 105–6
Butterscotch Pesto, 101

Cabbage:
  potatoes, and burgundy sauerkraut, with roast pork, 65
  red, in salad with pineapple, 32
Cake:
  Chocolate Truffle, 93
  devil's food, my grandma's, 110
  Upside-Down Tomato Cheese, 89
Calcium, 6
Candied Orange Slices, 106

Carrots:
  basic cooking technique for, 71
  in Curry Catsup, 72
  in Frangelico and Coffee, 72
  in Root Beer, 72
  sweet and sour, with bacon and onions, 72
Casaba melon, in Chicken Claret Soup, 27
Cashew, beet green, and havarti pesto, 83
Catsup, curry, with carrots, 72
Cauliflower Crown, 70
Celery:
  Knobs, Stuffed, 73
  Patties, 73
  Pudding, 73
Champagne:
  and Bacon Cream Sauce, 61–62, 96
  cream sauce, for turkey breast with crabmeat, 54–55, 96
  and Lobster Pate Cream Sauce, 52, 96
  and Radish Cream Soup, 25–26
  and raspberry vinegar, 35
  in sauces, 96
Cheddar:
  collard green, and pecan pesto, 82–83
  in fiddlehead fern pesto, 83
Cheese:
  custard, for smoked trout, 86
  and herbs, with baked tomatoes, 89
  and tomato cake, upside-down, 89
  See also Cheddar; Havarti; Jarlsberg; Muenster
Cheesecake:
  brandied pear, 107
  butterbrickle, a la Ippolito, 105–6
  chocolate nougat, with Frangelico, 105
  Cointreau, with candied orange slices, 106
  "formula," 104
  Pudding, 106–7
  white chocolate, with raspberries and creme de cassis, 105
Chicken:
  Breast with Beet Green Pesto and Brie, 47
  breast, sherried, with lobster tails and cheese, 47
  breast, sweet and sour, with mussels, 48
  Breast with Tofu, Mushrooms, and Zucchini, 81
  Claret with Casaba Melon Soup, 27
  Stir-Fry with Raisins and Sambuca Mayonnaise, 48

Chocolate:
  Almond Coffee, 111
  Nougat Cheesecake with Frangelico, 105
  Pesto, 101
  pesto, white, 101
  Truffle Cake, 93
  truffles, 93
Chowder:
  Artichoke Heart and Corn, 22
  Beet Green–Buttermilk, 22–23
  Ina Zwicker's Whitehead Island, 20–21
Chutney, cranberry, American style, 100
Cinnamon Orange Butter, 8
Clam broth, sherried, 28–29
Coffee:
  chocolate almond, 111
  and Frangelico with carrots, 72
Cognac:
  and Leek Sauce, 98
  Mushroom Sauce, 64
  and sour cream sauce, for striped bass, 40–41
  and tomato sauce, 41–42
Cointreau Cheesecake with Candied Orange Slices, 106
Cold Salmon in an Orange Custard Cream, 43, 99
Cold Smoked Mussels in Sour Cream and Onions, 16
Cold Smoked Mussels with Sauerkraut, 44
Collard Green, Pecan, and Cheddar Pesto, 82–83
Collards with bacon in stuffed sweet potatoes, 75
Conchs:
  preparation of, 17
  stuffed, 17
  where to buy, 17
Corn chowder, with artichoke hearts, 22
Crab:
  legs, and peaches, with bacon, yogurt, and chives, 32
  Meat, in One-Pot Fish Soup, 28
  meat sauce, sherried, 98
  meat, with striped bass, in cucumber sauce, 41
  meat, with turkey breast, in a champagne cream sauce, 54–55
  in Stuffed Sole in Tomato-Cognac Sauce, 41–42
Cranberry(ies):
  Chutney American Style, 100
  and Creme de Cassis Sauce, 49
  in Grand Marnier Sauce, 64–65
  swirl, curried, with sweet potatoes, 75

Cream:
    duxelle, for fillet of sole, 42
    heavy, in homemade butter, 6
    orange custard, 43
    orange-lobster, 42–43
Creamed Lobster with Artichoke
    Hearts, 43
Cream of Radish Soup, 25
Cream of Wild Rice Soup, 26
Cream soup base, 23
Crust, gardino, for pumpkin rosamond,
    107–8
Cucumber(s):
    and dandelion greens, 70–71
    salad, with apples and pineapple, 31
    sauce, 41, 102
    and Strawberries with Strawberry-
        Port Wine Vinegar, 32
Curried Asparagus Cream Soup, 24
Curried Duxelles in Brandy Topping, 16
Curried Green Tomatoes with Maple
    Syrup, 65
Curried Maple Syrup Dressing, 37, 99
Curried Pear Butter, 8
Curried Sweet Potato and Cranberry
    Swirl, 75
Curried Tomato–Sour Cream Sauce, 62–
    63
Curry:
    butter, sweet, 7–8
    catsup, for carrots, 72
Custard:
    brie, with artichoke hearts, 11
    cheese, for smoked trout, 86
    havarti and sherry, with artichoke
        hearts, 11
    orange, cream, 43, 99
    pear, for meringue pie, 109
    Tomato, 89

Dandelion greens:
    with black walnut dressing, 33
    and cucumbers, 70–71
Deep South Berwick Strawberries, 92
Dipped Asparagus, 91
Doughnuts, Indian, 9
Dressing:
    Black Olive and Sour Cream, 37, 99
    Black Walnut, 33
    Curried Maple Syrup, 37, 99
    Emerald City, 34
    Lemon-Pepper, 32, 36
    Pimiento and Sour Cream, 37, 99
    Raspberry-Honey, 31
    Strawberry and Honey, 37, 100

Duck, breast of:
    in blueberries and creme de cassis, 49
    in cranberries and creme de cassis, 49
    in grape leaves and grapefruit, 50
    in rhubarb and creme de cassis, 50
    stuffed into hot mangoes, 50–51
Duxelle(s), 12–13
    cream, for fillet of sole, 42
    curried, in brandy topping, 16
    with goose liver, 12–13
    in goose liver pate, 14

Eggplant and Tomatoes, 71
Eight-Minute Fish Stew, 85
Emerald City Dressing, 34
Emerald City Salad, 34, 85

Fast Spaghetti Sauce, 16, 84
Fiddlehead Fern:
    Pesto, 83
    pesto, in stuffed roast pork, 64
    soup, cream of, 23–24
Fillet of Sole:
    in Duxelle Cream, 42
    with Mussels in Sherry Butter, 42
Filo:
    with beef tenderloin, and shrimp and
        artichoke stuffing, 58–59
    with sweet and sour tenderloin pate,
        58
Fish:
    soup, 28
    stew, eight-minute, 85
    See also Bass; Haddock; Salmon;
        Shark; Shrimp; Sole; Trout; Tuna;
        Whitefish
French toast with wild strawberry
    butter, 7
Fricadelles, veal, with raisins, 66
Fried Apple Rings, 91
Fried Green Tomatoes, 90
Frogs' Legs in Lemon and Pimiento-
    Pernod Sauce, 44
Fruit, brandied winter, 100

Garlic Spinach Stuffing, 17
Garlic Butter Supreme, 8
Glaze, honey and cold duck, 97

Goose Liver(s):
    with Artichoke Hearts in a Cham-
        pagne and Bacon Sauce, 13–14
    in Cognac Cream Soup, 26
    in Cognac Cream with Duxelles, 12–13
    in Marmalade and Brandy Sauce, 13
    Pate, 14
    pate, with quail, in a cognac cream
        sauce, 53
Grapefruit:
    with breast of duck in grape leaves,
        50
    slices, with shredded zucchini, 31
Grape leaves for breast of duck, with
    grapefruit, 50

Haddock:
    with Langostinos in a White Wine-
        Parsley Sauce, 40
    in Plums and Brandy, 39–40
Ham, Sweet Potato, and Zucchini, 80–
    81
Hash, New England red flannel, 86
Havarti, in pesto, with beet greens and
    cashews, 83
Herb and May Wine Summer Cream
    Soup, 23, 99
Herbs:
    and cheese, with baked tomatoes, 89
    in folklore, 23
    medicinal properties of, 23
Honey and Cold Duck Glaze, 97
Hot Mangoes Stuffed with Duck, 50–51
Hot Sambuca Mayonnaise, 48, 99

Ina Zwicker's Whitehead Island
    Chowder, 20–21
Indian Doughnuts, 9

Jarlsberg, macadamia nut, and water-
    cress pesto, 83
Juniper berry and orange vinegar, 32, 35

Kirsch and Brandy Barbecue Sauce,
    87

Lamb:
  leg of, with curried green tomatoes,
    65
  Stir-Fry with Scallions and Pears, 66
Langostinos, with haddock, in a white
    wine–parsley sauce, 40
Leek and cognac sauce, 98
Leg of Lamb with Curried Green
    Tomatoes, 65
Lemon:
  Butter Cognac Sauce, 59, 99
  and Pepper Dressing, 32, 36
  and Pimiento-Pernod Sauce, 44
Lettuce, romaine, stuffed in trout, 85–
    86
Liqueurs, in butter, 7
Liver, goose. *See* Goose Liver(s)
Lobster and Havarti Cognac Cream
    Sauce, 81
Lobster:
  in butter, 7
  and champagne pate cream sauce, 52
  creamed, with artichoke hearts, 43
  in Ina Zwicker's Whitehead Island
    Chowder, 20–21
  in One-Pot Fish Soup, 28
  and orange cream sauce, 42–43
  -Orange Salad in Sambuca and Bacon
    Sour Cream, 43–44
  pate, for boned quail, 52
  in peach butter, 15–16
  tails and cheese, with sherried chicken
    breast, 47

Macadamia nut, watercress, and
    Jarlsberg pesto, 83
Mangoes:
  hot, stuffed with duck, 50–51
  and Smoked Salmon, 32–33
Maple syrup:
  in butter, 6
  with curried green tomatoes, 65
  dressing, curried, 37, 99
  with mustard, 18
  and tomato and Southern Comfort
    barbecue sauce, 95–96
Marmalade, orange, with Cointreau, for
    baked tomatoes, 74
Mayonnaise:
  hot, with Sambuca, 48, 99
  orange and bacon, 99
May wine, in herb and summer cream
    soup, 23, 99

Melon:
  casaba, in chicken claret soup, 27
  with Raw Salmon in a Ginger Sauce,
    33
Meringue, for pear custard pie, 109
Milk, skim, uses for, 6
Mint Butter, 8
Mousse, tofu, 92–93
Muenster in Fiddlehead Fern Pesto, 83
Mushroom(s):
  and bacon brandy sauce, 59–60
  in Cognac Sauce Flambe, 57–58
  tofu, and zucchini, with chicken
    breast, 81
  and vermouth sauce, 97
Mussels:
  cold smoked, with sauerkraut, 44
  cold smoked, in sour cream and
    onions, 16
  figuring number per person of, 15
  with fillet of sole, in sherry butter, 42
  preparation of, 15
  sherried, in cream soup, 21
  smoked, with quail and walnut
    cheese, in a champagne and lobster
    sauce, 51–52
  smoked, in sherried tomato soup, 22
  with sweet and sour chicken breast, 48
  toppings for, 15–16
My Grandma's Devil's Food Cake, 110

Nasturtium blossoms, 7
  in butter, 7
  with zucchini and spinach, 70
Nasturtium Salad, 34
New England Red Flannel Hash, 86
New England Sweet Potato Crown, 76
Nori:
  in sushi, 44–45
  in tomato clam broth with shrimp, 29
Nutmeg and Basil Butter, 8

Oils:
  flavoring, 36–37
  walnut-flavored, 36–37
Olives, black, and sour cream dressing,
    37
One-Pot Fish Soup, 28
Orange(s):
  and Bacon Mayonnaise, 99
  Brandy Sauce, 63

Orange(s), *continued*:
  Custard Cream, 43, 99
  and juniper berry vinegar, 32, 35
  and lobster cream sauce, 42–43
  and lobster salad, in Sambuca and
    bacon sour cream, 43–44
  marmalade, and Cointreau, with
    baked tomatoes, 74
  and raspberry sauce, for baked
    apples, 91
  slices, candied, 106
  with tarragon, anisette, and baked
    tomatoes, 90

Parsnip(s):
  and apples, with roast stuffed pork,
    64–65
  "Butter," 91
  Cakes, Shaker, 90
  Tugboat, 90–91
Pasta sauce:
  fast spaghetti, 84
  Lobster and Havarti Cognac Cream,
    81
  See also Pesto
Pate:
  goose liver, for quail, in a cognac
    cream sauce, 53
  lobster, for boned quail, 52
Peach(es):
  Brandy Barbecue Sauce, 96
  and crab legs, with bacon, yogurt,
    and chives, 32
  and lobster butter, 15–16
  and Sliced Radishes, 32
Peanut Butter:
  and Orange Soup, 24
  Sauce, 60, 102
Pear(s):
  in butter, 6
  curried, in butter, 8
  Custard Meringue Pie, 109
  and scallions, in lamb stir-fry, 66
Pecan, collard green, and cheddar pesto,
    82–83
Pesto:
  beet green, with brie, for chicken
    breast, 47
  Beet Green, Cashew, and Havarti, 82–
    83
  butterscotch, 101
  and cheese, for potatoes, 77
  chocolate, 101

continued

Pesto, *continued*:
    Fiddlehead Fern, 64, 83
    "formula" for, 83–84
    Spinach and Walnut, 82
    Watercress, Macadamia Nut, and
        Jarlsberg, 83
    white chocolate, 101
Pie:
    Pear Custard Meringue, 109
    Pumpkin Rosamund in a Gardino
        Crust, 107–8
    Tomato, 109
Pimiento and Sour Cream Dressing, 37,
    99
Pineapple:
    and Red Cabbage Salad, 32
    salad, with apple and cucumber, 31
Pizza, two-and-a-half-minute skillet, 88
Plum(s):
    and Cinnamon Port Wine Sauce, 98
    with brandy, for haddock, 39–40
Pork roast:
    with cabbage, potatoes, and burgundy
        sauerkraut, 65
    with fruit and sausage, in orange
        brandy sauce, 63
    stuffed with apples and parsnips, 64–
        65
    stuffed with fiddlehead fern pesto, 64
Port wine:
    sauce, with plums and cinnamon, 98
    and strawberry vinegar, 32, 35
Potatoes:
    with cheese and pesto, 77
    roast, in a bacon cream sauce, 76–77
Pudding:
    cheesecake, 106–7
    tofu-fruit, 92
Pumpkin Rosamund in a Gardino
    Crust, 107–8

Quail:
    boned, in a crown of lobster pate, 52
    with Goose Liver Pate in a Cognac
        Cream Sauce, 53
    with Walnut Cheese and Smoked
        Mussels in a Champagne and
        Lobster Sauce, 51–52, 96

Rabbit:
    Almandine in Mustard Maple Syrup,
        18
    in Orange Barbecue Sauce, 18
    preparation of, 18

Radish(es):
    champagne and, cream soup, 25–26
    shredded white, with sliced orange, 32
    sliced, with peaches, 32
    soup, cream of, 25
Raspberry:
    and champagne vinegar, 35
    and honey dressing, 31
    and orange sauce, for baked apples,
        91
Ratatouille, 70
Red cabbage salad, with pineapple, 32
Rhubarb and Creme de Cassis Sauce, 50
Rice, wild. *See* Wild rice
Roast Leg of Veal in a Champagne and
    Bacon Cream Sauce, 61–62
Roast Pork:
    with Cabbage, Potatoes, and
        Burgundy Sauerkraut, 65
    with Fruit and Sausage in Orange
        Brandy Sauce, 63
    Stuffed with Apples and Parsnips,
        64–65
    Stuffed with Fiddlehead Fern Pesto,
        64
Root beer, with carrots, 72

Salad:
    Apple, Pineapple, and Cucumber, 31
    Bacon, Yogurt, and Chives on
        Peaches and Crab Legs, 32
    Cucumbers and Strawberries with
        Strawberry–Port Wine Vinegar, 32
    Dandelion Greens with Black Walnut
        Dressing, 33
    Emerald City, 34
    lobster-orange, in Sambuca and
        bacon sour cream, 43–44
    Mangoes and Smoked Salmon, 32–33
    Melon with Raw Salmon in a Ginger
        Sauce, 33
    Nasturtium, 34
    Peaches and Sliced Radishes, 32
    Pineapple and Red Cabbage, 32
    Shredded White Radish and Sliced
        Orange, 32
    Shredded Zucchini and Grapefruit
        Slices in Raspberry-Honey
        Dressing, 31
    Spinach and Bacon Cognac Caesar,
        33
    Sweet and Sour Apples, Bacon, and
        Zucchini, 31

Salmon:
    with Artichoke in Orange-Lobster
        Cream, 42–43
    bisque, baked, 21
    cold, in orange custard cream, 43
    raw, with melon in a ginger sauce, 33
    smoked, with mangoes, 32–33
Sambuca:
    and bacon sour cream, for lobster-
        orange salad, 43–44
    baked tomatoes in, with lemon herb
        butter, 74
    herb butter, with raisins in chicken
        stir-fry, 48
    mayonnaise, hot, 48
Sauces:
    bacon cream, for roast potatoes, 76–
        77
    Bacon and Mushroom Brandy, 59–60
    barbecue, with tomato, Southern
        Comfort, and maple, 95–96
    Blueberries and Creme de Cassis, 49
    champagne and bacon, 13–14
    champagne and bacon cream, 61–62,
        96
    champagne cream, for turkey breast,
        with crabmeat, 54–55, 96
    Champagne and Lobster Pate Cream,
        52, 96
    cognac cream, for quail with goose
        liver pate, 53
    Cognac and Leek, 98
    Cranberries and Creme de Cassis, 49
    Cranberry Grand Marnier, 64–65
    Cucumber, 41
    Curried Tomato–Sour Cream, 62–63
    Fast Spaghetti, 16, 84
    Ginger, 33
    Kirsch and Brandy Barbecue, 87, 95
    Lemon Butter Cognac, 59, 99
    Lemon and Pimiento-Pernod, 44
    Lobster and Havarti Cognac Cream,
        81
    marmalade and brandy, 13
    Mushroom Cognac, Flambe, 57–58
    Orange Barbecue, 18
    Orange Brandy, 63
    Orange-Lobster Cream, 42–43
    Peanut Butter, 60, 102
    Plum and Cinnamon Port Wine, 98
    Raspberry-orange, for baked apples,
        91
    Rhubarb and Creme de Cassis, 50
    Sambuca Barbecue, 88, 95
    simple butter, with wine, 99
    sour cream, 73

continued

Sauces, *continued:*
  Sweet and Sour Tomato, 58
  Tomato-Cognac, 41–42
  Vermouth-Mushroom, 97
  Walnut-Cheese, 67
  White Vermouth Cream, 68, 97
  White Wine–Parsley, 40, 97
  White Wine and Sour Cream
    Paprika, 97
  See also Cream; Dressing; Pate

Sauerkraut:
  burgundy, with cabbage and potatoes,
    for roast pork, 65
  with cold smoked mussels, 44
Sausage, and fruit, with roast pork, in
  orange brandy sauce, 63
Scallops:
  in Ina Zwicker's Whitehead Island
    Chowder, 20–21
  in One-Pot Fish Soup, 28
  and striped bass, in a cognac–sour
    cream sauce, 40–41
Seafood in a Sherried Clam Broth, 28–
  29
Seaweed. *See* Nori
Shaker cooking, 25–26, 27
Shaker Parsnip Cakes, 90
Shark Janis Paige, 85
Sherried Chicken Breast with Lobster
  Tails and Cheese, 47
Sherried Crabmeat Sauce, 98
Sherried Mussel Cream Soup, 21
Sherry:
  and almond vinegar, 36
  and black walnut vinegar, 32, 35
  Butter, 42
Shredded White Radish and Sliced
  Orange, 32
Shrimp:
  and Artichoke Stuffing, 59
  in tomato clam broth with nori, 29
Simple Butter Sauce with Wine, 99
Smoked Mussels in Sherried Tomato
  Cream, 21–22
Smoked Trout in a Cheese Custard, 86
Sole:
  crab-stuffed, in tomato-cognac sauce,
    41–42
  in duxelle cream, 42
  fillet of, with mussels, in sherry
    butter, 42
Soup:
  artichoke heart and corn chowder, 22
  Baked Salmon Bisque, 21
  Beet Green–Buttermilk Chowder, 22–
    23
  champagne and radish cream, 25

Soup, *continued:*
  Chicken Claret with Casaba Melon,
    27
  cream-based, 23
  cream of fiddlehead fern, 23–24
  cream of radish, 25
  cream of wild rice, 26
  curried asparagus cream, 24
  goose livers in cognac cream, 26
  Herb and May Wine Summer Cream,
    23, 99
  Ina Zwicker's Whitehead Island
    Chowder, 20–21
  medicinal uses of, 27
  One-Pot Fish, 28
  peanut butter and orange, 24
  Seafood in a Sherried Clam Broth,
    28–29
  Sherried Mussel Cream, 21
  Smoked Mussels in Sherried Tomato
    Cream, 22
  Tomato Clam Broth with Shrimp and
    Nori, 29
  Vatican vichyssoise, 24
Sour cream:
  and black olive dressing, 37, 99
  and cognac sauce, for striped bass, 37
  and curried tomato sauce, 62–63
  and pimiento dressing, 37, 99
  with Sambuca and bacon, for lobster-
    orange salad, 43–44
  sauce, 73
  and white wine paprika sauce, 97
Spinach:
  and Bacon Cognac Caesar, 33
  and Walnut Pesto, 82
  and zucchini, with nasturtiums, 70
Stir-fry:
  chicken, with raisins and Sambuca
    mayonnaise, 48
  lamb, with scallions and pears, 66
Strawberry(ies):
  and black pepper topping, 15
  and cucumbers, 32
  Deep South Berwick, 92
  and Honey Dressing, 37, 100
  and port wine vinegar, 32, 35
  wild, with French toast, 7
Striped Bass:
  in a Cognac–Sour Cream Sauce, with
    Scallops, 40–41
  with Crabmeat in Cucumber Sauce,
    41
Stuffed Celery Knobs, 73
Stuffed Conchs, 17

Stuffing:
  apple, 87
  garlic spinach, 17
  shrimp and artichoke, 59
Sushi, 44–45
Sweet Curry Butter, 7–8
Sweet Pickle, Anchovy, and Green
  Chartreuse Topping, 15
Sweet Potato(es):
  Crown, New England, 76
  with ham and zucchini, 80–81
  Stuffed with Bacon and Collards, 75
  swirl, curried, with cranberries, 75
Sweet and Sour:
  Apples, Bacon, and Zucchini Salad,
    31
  Chicken Breast with Mussels, 48
  Green Fried Tomatoes, 74
  Tenderloin Pate in Filo, 58
  Tomato Sauce, 58

Tenderloin, beef. *See* Beef
Tofu:
  with chicken breast, mushrooms, and
    zucchini, 81
  and fruit pudding, 92
  Mousse, 92–93
Tomato(es):
  Baked in Herbs and Cheese, 89
  baked in orange marmalade, with
    Cointreau, 74
  Baked in Orange with Tarragon and
    Anisette, 90
  baked in Sambuca and lemon herb
    butter, 74
  and cheese cake, upside-down, 89
  Clam Broth with Shrimp and Nori, 29
  and cognac sauce, 41–42
  curried, and sour cream sauce, 62–63
  curried green, with maple syrup, 65
  custard, 89
  with eggplant, 71
  fried green, 74, 90
  pie, 109
  sherried, cream soup, 21–22
Topping for mussels:
  brandy, with curried duxelles, 16
  strawberry-black pepper, 15
  sweet pickle, anchovy, and green
    chartreuse, 15
Trout:
  smoked, in cheese custard, 86
  stuffed with Romaine, 85–86
Truffles, chocolate, 93

continued

Tugboat Parsnips, 90–91
Tuna:
    roast, in beet greens, 39
    Steaks in Olive Oil and Honey, 38–39
Turkey:
    Breast in a Champagne Cream Sauce
        with Crabmeat, 54–55, 96
    Meltdown, 54
Two-and-a-Half-Minute Skillet Pizza, 88

Upside-Down Tomato Cheese Cake,
    89

Vatican Vichyssoise, 24
Veal:
    Cutlets Stuffed with Apple in a
        Walnut-Cheese Sauce, 67
    Cutlets Stuffed with Artichoke and
        Pimiento, 67–68
    Fricadelles with Raisins, 66
    in goose liver pate, 14
    Roast in a Curried Tomato–Sour
        Cream Sauce, 62–63
    roast leg of, in a champagne and
        bacon cream sauce, 61–62

Vermouth-Mushroom Sauce, 97
Vichyssoise, Vatican, 24
Vinegar:
    Almond-Sherry, 36
    Lemon-Pepper, 36
    making your own, 35
    Orange–Juniper Berry, 32, 35
    Raspberry-Champagne, 35
    Sherry–Black Walnut, 33, 35
    Strawberry–Port Wine, 32, 35

Walnut:
    black, and sherry vinegar, 33, 35
    and cheese sauce, 67
    -flavored oil, 36–37
    and spinach pesto, 82
Watercress, Macadamia Nut, and Jarls-
    berg Pesto, 83
White Chocolate:
    Cheesecake with Raspberries and
        Creme de Cassis, 105
    Pesto, 101

Whitefish, in Ina Zwicker's Whitehead
    Island Chowder, 20–21
White Vermouth Cream Sauce, 68, 97
White Wine and Sour Cream Paprika
    Sauce, 97
White Wine–Parsley Sauce, 40, 97
Wild rice:
    guidelines for preparation of, 77–78
    soup, cream of, 26

Yogurt, bacon, and chives on peaches
    and crab legs, 32

Zucchini:
    with ham and sweet potato, 80–81
    salad, with sweet and sour apples and
        bacon, 31
    shredded, with grapefruit slices, 31
    and spinach with nasturtiums, 70
    tofu, and mushrooms, with chicken
        breast, 81

If you'd like one or more copies of James Haller's first bestselling book, *The Blue Strawbery Cookbook: Cooking (Brilliantly) Without Recipes,* write:

The Harvard Common Press
Department CC
535 Albany Street
Boston, Massachusetts o2118

The Blue Strawbery Cookbook is available in a clothbound edition for $12.50 and a paperback edition for $8.95. When ordering, enclose a check or money order for the full price plus $2.00 for postage and handling. If you are a Massachusetts resident, please add 5 percent sales tax.

The Harvard Common Press also publishes several other cookbooks. We'd be happy to send you our catalog at no charge. Just write us at the above address.